WINTER MARIA:

POEMS OF SAINTHOOD, MOTHERHOOD, & UNLIKELIHOODS

John David Thompson

CONTACT POET @
iowapoems175@yahoo.com or at FACEBOOK Blue Jay's Bungalow Press

"Nobody will write a book…about my mother—"

President Richard Milhous Nixon, Resignation Speech
August 9, 1974

FOR MARJORIE MARIE

BORN ON THE CUSP OF WINTER

WINTER MARIA

WINTER MARIA:
POEMS OF SAINTHOOD, MOTHERHOOD, & UNLIKELIHOODS

ISBN 978-1-7328665-0-8

LIBRARY OF CONGRESS CONTROL NUMBER: 2018911909

All poems written by John David Thompson; some poems may have appeared in previous publication(s) by author.

Graphic Artwork and Electronic Layout by Karisa Runkel

MANUFACTURED IN THE UNITED STATES OF AMERICA
BLUE JAY'S BUNGALOW PRESS
TO CONTACT POET: e-mail @ iowapoems175@yahoo.com or
FACEBOOK / BLUE JAY'S BUNGALOW PRESS

POEMS FOR *WINTER MARIA: POEMS OF SAINTHOOD, MOTHERHOOD, & UNLIKELIHOODS*

PROLOGUE

Winter Maria

Lowly,
I prefer my angels,

lowly like a swinging chariot,
with me like mittens through winter

tending to exposed delicacies—
breaking winds and bones.

The season itself
stirs like a campestral cat—

all troubles and yarns,
implausible stories and strings.

Yes,
I need something lowly

to ground me
among such makeshift wings.

It is she, Winter Maria;
her frame clears

before the slag-furnace dross,
imperial debris,

maternal as milk,
ethereal balance,

offering bulbs of snowdrops in one hand,
Lenten roses, upon the other.

Her gracious labor arrives
—on wistful, pleated arms—

Born from still wind, same blessing
that delivered Our Savior,

she, the one
who has found God's favor.

POEMS OF SAINTHOOD

Bernadette of Lourdes

It was in a grotto,
a cave of thrown shadow, refuse, remains.
(Why I was there?
I cannot but meditate.)

I had gone to gather firewood—
departed, garnered in Immaculate Faith.

My impoverished skin
stood still
as the lowing stone—
then a pledge of water,
a spring to unseal winter's
disbelieving conjuring.

I spied in silence,
a faculty of white.
When it spoke, oh—
the language of such living light.

Whom rang through me
like a shrill river,
then—this quivering bell.

Whom to trust? Whom to abandon?
Whom to abide? Whom to tell?

All of Lourdes discovered the crags and faults.
Lanterned tongues flamed our cliff-born tête-à-tête.

This is a pilgrim's shrine now.

Sails and stakes imprint,
interpret visions—
Virgin Mother and miller saint

who lift each wandered spirit
like tides from heaven—
but never drift away.

Saints

During his resignation
one teary-sealed August, noon-swoon,
President Richard Milhous Nixon
committed an egregious error
of the grammatical, grandiose kind.

He babble-stained that his mother was a saint.

Carrying the shame of a nation
on his lugubrious, lachrymose shoulders,
slobbering over prime-time airwaves
like Lucy pout-pitching for another audition
at Ricky's Club Babalu,
Tricky Dick put the hagiographical existence
of Mother Hannah in the past tense.

His leadership like his maternal loyalty
remains in question.

You see, my mother *is* a saint.
Prior to infant flesh, as she walks this earth,
after this momentary air of passing through—

I do not have to betray a republic
to share, hereafter, she *is* a saint.

Neither death nor my public humiliation
can ever deny her goodness in eternal presence.

My mother *is* a saint, and so, it seems, Richard, is yours.
And I will write terse,
but loving verse-books about both women and their ilk—

And the pen is pure.

First Corinthians—The Gift of Love (13: 1-13)

It is the beautiful truism of soul and ceremony,
a seal-kiss letter descending from heaven
open to an unwritten page.

It is the antidote to everything nothing.

It knows what knowledge cannot comprehend.

It has gathered the nameless, united the shameful.

Even garland hope, petaled promises are mere attendants
to its immaculate veil.

It rids the sanctuary of sin, wants no other spiritual gift.

It is the final arrangement to every invitation.

It refuses to speak to hellish fear or worldly reason.

Its weapon waits with wide disarmament—and a daisy-forgiving grin.

Love never forfeits; it possesses no linen to toss into a puckish arena.

It encourages the child, admonishes the childish.

It weathers, suffers, and endures.
Still, it runs thoroughly a-pace upon a ceaseless course.
It is bred to selfless roses.

It will hold the mirror of revelation, diminish lesser light—
reunite faces to God, fill and clarify the last vacating vapors.

When all on earth is hesitant, then gone—
It will share eternity's room
with hope and faith.

But the residency of Love will be greater.

The Invention of Angels

Because God is a Maker—
and these winged fathoms
stand as glorious ghost dolls
in His image-house—
remedial intermediaries—
the busy, undutiful children cannot see them
or their myriad of miracles.

Ah, the young, and the not-so-young—
their curious hands and minds
create driven stories and flesh settings
with shortcomings, salt-riveting faults
for which grit spirits must shore.

The Lord is First Carpenter,
Head Mattock in the Attic,
yet distant in discourse from ordinary reach.

The angels are His work and wonder,
mystery and manifestation,
magnificent couriers,
tell-tales in a meditative wind
reminding our sins and psyches
just that: it takes work and wonder.

Hammered to heal, gilded to guide,
crafted and clayed to protect,
willed to shield everything from us—
except our free will,

angels are the intelligent, immaculate
proofs on the roof,
feathers of encouraging faith,
blessed friends to our old souls,
bearers of the final, floating pall,
heavenly hosts to escort us
to comfort in waiting cosmos, awakening…a-far.

And their winks of approval are the twinkling stars.

Hagiography 101

The study of saints is no bed of rosaries.
Rules and rituals pertaining to the glorious goners
appear and erect
as evanescent as a glimpse
of heaven.

Catholics, these days, prefer their hallows dead,
performing a miracle or two to prove canonized-worthy—overhead.
Oh, martyrdom on earth still applies,
an underage soldier a-flame, hanging arcs of ashes
in a gallows-sky.

Peter as first saint at the gate has remained a universal pearl.
Paul was shamed by Jesus into one, on the road to Damascus.
The Dominicans and Franciscans were pious street gangs of sorts.

Write a compare/contrast essay about each order, then pray to St. Anthony—
in case you lost the report.

Saints Thomas Aquinas, Augustine, and Bonaventure
clung to theological philosophy like static hooks.
Patrick instructed the pagan pubs of Ireland
about the Holy Trinity
using the shamrock as symbolic flute to the Good Book.

St. Therese of Lisieux, the Little Flower, read souls,
then offered lowered ones a lift.
St. Pio revealed Christ's wounds in a modern man's hand.
Pope John Paul II proclaimed Luminous Mysteries
to be garlanded among meditative rifts.

Practice, bent-beaded ones, on your own.

Witness the saints for shoes, saints for hats,
saints for this, and saints for that.
Do not confuse saints for angels who guide the course—
but not required to take it, my marching-in scholars.
Budding saints must enroll, endure—just like you, then bloom with cloud-high colors.

Sonnet of the Angels

Distant creations—before fire, fury
Sanctuaries on wing to serve earth-trod
Courtiers of praise, each promise from God
Jesus alongside, amicus curiae

Temptation's churl calls on the weary
Machiavellian truths in tongues of fraud
Angels enter foul scheme to clear cloud-sod
Triumph's verdict dismisses Satan's jury

Ecclesiastic abstracts, healing harps
Magnificent muses lent to your ear
Advisors of love, peace to all nations

Messengers, protectors—works of fine art
Tided, wrestle-worn, passage without peer
Marked from *Genesis to Revelation*

Paul-The Prison Epistles

PROLOGUE

Spirit housed in darkness, drunk with light,
we walk together with faith and hope in these chained letters.

EPHESIANS

Among these quiet, captive stones,
I encourage you to prepare for battle.
Salvation is not for you to hail, but to cherish.
Grace has surged, swayed, and saved you
in a sea's whisper.
Be still, soldiers, so that you sense all schemes.
Armor yourselves with garments of truth.
Take this helmet to heart.
Ready your feet with foundation, the gospel of peace.

PHILIPPIANS

Held in Rome, I am held in joy, gratitude, and thankfulness,
this thrice-weaving bond I release to the people of Philippi.
This slant of light, humility's illume, I share with you.
Hunger of plenty, abundant need—we seal in this letter,
the same love, same mind.
In this low dwelling, I am kept high by your burgeoning belief,
higher in Christ's passing, highest in His coming.
The wounds of imprisonment flow from this healing reed.
Containment has taught me contentment, and I am daily freed.

PAUL-THE PRISON EPISTLES

COLOSSIANS

With scant light and water, I am still rooted, bearing fruit
to you in words of His preeminent wisdom until our first meeting.
Your hearts must feel much more than any lips can say.
Glorious is simplicity,
for what can be added to Christ's labors on the cross?
Nothing.
Wade not in the flesh spirits of shallow tongues.
Any man who wakes can claim he has been other-ways saved.
Tell the false teacher to put a nail on it, then re-sing it from the grave.

PHILEMON

I write to you in the hand of friendship,
illiterate of authority, apostolic craft.
An unbeliever, unprofitable slave arrived at my chamber,
myself a prisoner of Christ.
Any crime or debt this Onesimus has incurred on your property,
steal away the theft, transfer all cost, burden's breath to me.
I am suggesting this as your brother, who, in turn,
sends this visitor back to you—a brother redeemed.
Let all hierarchy come to heel. Let forgiveness heal.

Liberation of St. Peter by Raphael, Apostolic Palace, Vatican City

The latticework of the Mamertinum iron bars,
a kind of net, cast like a stone trawl,
not so much excavating but captivating
the sea bottom endurance of a pent St. Peter.

Lumbering garments of the prison guards
ignite each to tire, unhinge in exchanges
of chained repose.

Enter the lave shape and light
of an angel, nameless intermediary,
bound by God, to set all about—boundless.

It is as if the witnessing moonlight
promises not tell, a twine
between the will of heaven,
works of this earth.

The feign stairs of broad Palladian fresco
offer nothing but mock staging
compared to the rise, revise—
Divine Providence softly unfurls.

In the far-right triptych,
First Bishop is free.
Heavy night rejoices in quiet Hallelujahs.

Clouds above Rome, hushed collects,
in pillor and color

of gated pearl—

Saint Luke

All of Greece is in debt
to the physician's mending hands,
medicine for the soul,
his epistle-palette
of evangelical paints,
testament to the Virgin's call,
humility's journey, magi mount
for unto us is born a Child
written, examined
in such pensive, lyric account.

All of Greece listens.
The ears and urns, bent still
to what he told to Theophilus
by tongue of eyewitness,
his companionship with Paul,
through prisons of Rome,
parable-passages, and quill.

Greece reads and is moved
by God's doctor and author
of denizen horizons and Christian lands,
the heralded historian who adhered
to the Lord's letter—
this articulation of good news
recounting what heals and redeems
for unseen star-voyage travails
of both Gentile and Jew.

Short Story of Ruth

What am I but a wrestle-worn refugee,
retracing the steps of Bethlehem's daughter?

Death's famine has reaped, cleared our fruited family.

And so my mother-in-law, Naomi,
returns to replenished Israel,
without structure of husband, company of sons.

Trialed, I can only give her true word:
to go and to follow.

I walk behind the stately woman,
gathering barley and darkness,
reaping the spared sheaves
as cast horizon harvests the sun.

I learn to watch the fields, the men
who know how to master the green offerings.

Boaz, who holds the land and its measure,
is kind to me. He permits me to drink
from the water jar. I sustain through
the parched settlings of days.

The family reshapes as a cloud from heaven.

I fall to thresher floor upon Boaz' feet in gratitude.
Bitter travesties of the past winnow in the waking wind.

The land of Naomi's people is repurchased, reclaimed.
Boaz and I, in time, consummate private provisions.

This is a story of small acts—footsteps, grains, good deeds, favors.

Troubling loss may cleave at our courage, but loyalty is the thing.

I will bear this in mind until I am buried in Christian soils that would not forsake us—

leaving behind a lineage of Old and New Testament kings.

—for Kathleen Evenhouse

Hannah's Lament

It is useless to confess
how I am suffering
without risking
the tenacity and tone
of a thankless rose.

Yet, I have bloomed
into nothing, mocked
by the boast aggressions
of such fertile fields.

There is a confidence
in such yearning, a heartbeat
that is not my own.
It brings me here, knee-drawn,
pounding a prayer, fervid supplication
in obedient want of a child.

Do I dare submit,
why not? He is yours.

Alas, I am voiceless.
This is sound from a grieving interior,
stem-empty landscape,
in need of something to raise,
someone to love.

The morning light ascends
like a spread jury, barren—
of direct answer.

Lord, you are first wisdom.
Let my unborn appeal serve as last judge.

Job's Suffering

You millennials, echo boomers,
might relate best to me
as a disenfranchised quarterback, company clown—
blindsided brother, who never saw it coming.

At least, you are given the dramatic irony
forsaken to me—
God held council with Satan
who dared Our Father to strip me
of all rings, endurances—to see what I could,
indeed, ring-of-fire endure.

I will tell you this: bad news travels fast.

I did not invent the relentless, teeming wheel,
much less propagate its ravenous path.

If I grew it, raised it, or fathered it—
it was in a banish-breath—gone.

My first wife vacated once my body prostituted
a brothel of boils.

Where was the Lord, my protector?
I could not question without firing bronze pellets of blame.

Surrounded by miserable comforters,
I rendered, retarded by their quick philosophies to explain:
sin, test, or God's plan.

Innocence stood, not relieved by such sideshow explanations.

Faith resided under my skin,
suspended—homeless, hopeless to abandon it
whatever heaven's will.

This is my submission in the spin of such a wicked exhibition.

The world is still not fair.
All the world's a fair—still.

Solemnity of Mary

First day in January

When the angel behaved before her,
she drown
in a slave-sea of mankind's sins,
on the salted chains toward a breaded town.

Those were her disbelieving eyes,
grievous stone and sunk-shallow,
humble to a doubt.
This was the first silent night.
Airless, beating with Heaven's heart,
her lungs told no one,
even husband Joseph toiled with her fruit labors,
with such brute incredulity.

What else was there to do
but tax-travel, sand-toe and sojourn
for unfathomable, footed miles?
She'd go anywhere, boot anywhere
on the back of a donkey,
on the back of a hack vision,
no self-righteous Israelite professed to see.

Are we not her genesis-jury,
the ones left in posterity,
seated revelation-high,
for three or four generations,
before we done-die,
to decide the withers of her shouldered weather,
if she kept swaddle, saddle, and song
in the comprehensible all-togethers?

Our Lord either made or laid her,
a breath's way from both—or blaspheme;
we, nonetheless, observe—be it pastoral or perverse,
meek and mild, even or odd.
Mary appears to the sum of some—
Mother of God.

The Beatitudes

Not the threat of punishment,
but glint offering of gold reward—
this is cause for me, His Son,
to mount, stand upon this high stone
before you the lowly, blessed lowly.

The Lord is there with you,
granting you fullness, protection
asking only bread effort.

Does this moral ground want for weakness?
Do I reflect the passing rains of a shallow storm?
This is not a rock-toss of commandments,
but a tendering caress.

You who speak, want, work, and crave—
you are right to thrive below the worldly standard,
survive despite the wicked, rising bar.

How high must the rose rise to beautify, abide?

Consider the cowering, the hovering, the darkening,
the doomed. Walk with the weary.

Blessed be the eternal whim to be kind.

You are about to embark on a journey
of numbers, fractures, craven endeavors.

I never gathered you at the bank-grove to collect coin-olives.

Idleness is temptation of the spirit, not the harmless hand.

The sun spreads its mercy, meditation, light to take you to devout ways.

Tacit observers will be heard.

You, too, are my disciples,
learning the art of waiting, forgiving, humble living.

This is my earthly message and passage to Heaven's Word.

Joan of Arc

My hour of death came long
before these galloping flames sought
the Rouen accused, blazing Maid of Orleans
dowsed in such heretic smoke.

Indeed, I wore armor,
for I was no longer
among the godless living—
yet, a silver scape upon
a death-encrusted horse.

When the saints spoke,
a gate opened.
Earth faltered,
or confessed,

it was fallen all along.

My ride was with illiterate time,
disenfranchised, immune
to the discrepancy
of victory, defeat.

At last, I testified in earned ash,
learned, burning hundred-year-old tongue—
Give France to France
trial served,
terror done.

Entwined to wood
for wearing a soldier's hood,
I widened my tired thighs
for fire's licking place—

a lighted candle,
heaved to heaven
by history and histrionics'
mistaken, quickened pace.

Martyrdom

Santo Subido, Sainthood Now

A martyr does not die for a cause.

Agony need not wake each day,
walk nearer to damnation's flame.

To suffer is not to exterminate
what is surviving light
against a vaulted, star-gone gaze.

Most martyrs I know are alive;
they burn
from a pulse-giving heart;
it breathes, drawn,
not so much by invidious war
but toward the dawning immortality
of art.

A martyr does not say kill me,
but paint me
in flickers of hope,
those feathers that seed
human beings when wing-erect.

No, a martyr does not die for cause.

A martyr lives for effect.

Saint Augustine

Yes, I confess
I told you that you could build
a ladder with your vices—
quite similar in construct
to my own upward braiding;
but there was assumption,
a granted understanding
to involve mind, body, and soul—
a natural tendency, virginal leniency
toward heaven.

I can see now
that centuries mired
in humankind's wanton pools
has left you pitted
with foolishness, fanaticism.

What common objects these are,
your hourly events, roundabout excursions
creating nothing more than distance
from your Deity.

I thought my trod experiences,
libertine lessons could be transferred,
meditated upon, then serve as tools
to make you an architect of angels.

Each word, this passage
seem to fall like broken echoes
upon your inverted ways.

Downward, I toss
this cloth, wisp covenant of the Gospel,
to cool and comfort you
upon approach to such bottomless blaze.

St. Lucia, Patroness of the Blind

Here, take these eyes—on this Pontius plate
if they will assist the Roman Empire
to see the catastrophes spurned
on Christians, civilians of Sicily.

What has our God, our Savior
condemned onto you except resignation on cross,
resurrection through stone?

It is the mystery, isn't it—
bone command of the unknown?
The inexplicable thin-air rise
to a place no Augustus, no Nero,
momentary throne-hero could ever rule.

Your edicts permit the North Africans
to worship Saturn, the tribes of Jews
to foot at Jehovah temples.
Why even the archaic Greeks are allowed
to institute Zeus.

I cannot be obliged to where I am not committed.
My father's bread, I have given to the poor who pass.

Perhaps it is this amulet of light, crown of candles
I possess, you fear.
Your armor-clad guards, cumbersome oxen
attempt to drag me—to a brothel,
stake my reputation to damnation,
set my faith to flame.

Winter seeks as if first witness,
this longest night of a most perpetual, dark year.

The sword is cursed cold.
A relevance of angels speaks my enlightened name.

Eye for eye, blind to blind.
It is nothing, if not all in the same.

—for Heather

St. Valentine of Terni

When rose scales fall on winter's plagues of white,
Dark dulcets of passion stow in a box,
When top hats court sheer scarves down private locks,
The blood of St. Valentine lends its smite.

Good saint lost his head uniting others.
Defying laws of Claudius the Cruel,
The holy martyr willed impulses' fuel,
Dissident gift, knots tying banned lovers.

And so the libertine leaps, counts the ways—
Romance deepens, broadens, lengthens our light.
Sappho's sand letters cling—unembellished.
Long burn Casanova, *Kama Sutra's* blaze.
We receive the heart's card, Cupid's delights.
Blessed red sin, sorrows, stains—we relish.

St. Catherine of the Wheel

It has become a mad,
perhaps fabricated quiddity
between martyrdom and myth—
whether I hung low on tall tongues
or did exist.

Sea of breaches,
mystic Mediterranean,
born from a tempest ocean,
I speak from the Pharos Lighthouse,
your glowing port.

Rome has expanded like a plague;
it darkens shackled streets, harbors
to haunt the soul.

I am a captive
as the city itself, fallen Alexandria—
in ruins for the witness
to resurrecting word of Christ.

Maxentius thirsts for Africa.
He feeds us to lions for the clawing continent.

Here is the fierce wheel
upon which I am to succumb,
weave my limbs like lamb's wool
to break before the empire
as if my Christian witness were to cave
to the fraying gods to come.

Angels roll in with late tides,
wash erring atmosphere clean.
Whatever ebbs to deity's end
justifies flotsam, merciful shattering
of wicked means.

Saint Benedict

If anything,
I am the Patron Saint of Paradox—
the more I learned of Rome's matter, rich materials—
the less I sought its ephemeral rewards.

In isolation,
I planned for a community, Grand Monastery
a gathering of monks
to speak of the Spirit in silence.

And the miracles—
how ordinary their hooks and handles—
earthenware repaired,
a man's dissolute life drowned.

At Monte Cassino,
I built as I plundered—
hedonistic villages of doubt
each bearing bastard palms, pagan flame.

In short,
I could elaborate about my rules, further teachings,
but that would be based on the wisdom of ignorance.
Sin knows what its hands are doing. Shame. Shame.

St. Anthony of Padua

Tell me what you fear,
for in fear is forbearance
of loss.

You appear in object-want
of discovery, finding,
yet slip to see
the soul is on crusade
listing to reclaim
some holy realm
meant to crib, steady humanity.

Pray to me if you will, but
your heart is where you left it,
beating its breadcrumbs
to lead you
toward a passage, home.

Nothing here magnifies.

I am spy-human,
observer, perhaps teacher.
Still, you pray as if
I had wings
to unlatch
all of heaven's golden locks,
pinnate codes.

Something key to deem, I suppose,
always there,
wind-born, feather-rigid
sky and air—
bewildering breath
like a truant mood.

It is hope,
unearthed and leavened,
here if only
gone for good.

Jude Descending the Titanic Grand Staircase

After X. J. Kennedy's Nude Descending a Staircase

Break upon break, a salted flesh
With club of flame and leaded mind,
St. Jude sifts through flotsam, down drowning stairs
To congregate prayers for the foundered, left-behind.

He spies beneath carved banister
To witness God's will and wash on high rise;
He dips an offering, eternal air
To the nostril-pooled and floating passers-by.

Apostle-Waterfall, he wears
A rare drapery of heroic seaweed, ocean mosses
To rope the hopeless from frosted sea—
This blessed saint of lost causes.

St. Michael, the Archangel

A brace wind itself should tell you,
warn you, there are foes in this world,
breaks against the rowing boat,
stroking heart, glory's will upon high.

How can I help you
if you do not bend like a crown-laden willow
at head and heel,
not in subordination or deference,
but toward testimonial respect,
common sense, resource,
self-salvation?

It begins here, atop this crusted mantle,
this spinning blue opal in wave-stasis,
dizzying rise of a steadfast sun.

For God's sake, accord yourself.
Each waking hour is funnel-full,
replete with possibility, atonement, a mistral of prayer.

I am old and tested.
What if I, too, become temperamental?

If I am like God,
what, then, is to become of my patient wrath?

Here is my aegis, my ministry,
this willingness to be present
when your breath falls to composites of earth.

The end is its own rivalry,
waiting battle, cliché' in feigned amazement,
holding the psalmist's tea leaves,
the proverbalist's cards.

What if I am winging it, making this up;
what if it's seraphim, full-of-it stuff?

Tomorrow's blunt blows to sharpen or weaken you,
like resurrecting, down trades are suggestion enough.

St. Francis of Assisi

If I speak,
let it be bird-speak,
a still word with the tern,
delivery among gladsome doves.

It is not that I bend
my staff against humans
eye-toothing for silver sustenance
from well-empty souls.

My affair with poverty
grows to betrothed commitment;
the glorious want of nothing
suits my tattered sandal and wool.

Something has lifted,
from the lower faculties
of my resident being—homeless, hopeful
grateful enemy of earthen desire.

Its rise commands order,
this following of friars—
ropes and robes united,
deprived of mercantile strings.

How can I attest,
explain this strange madness
to the whipping boys
of the fisted, florin-coin rising?

Perhaps it is best
to confess, at first,
to the white-breasted throat,
a contented free wing.

—for the nightbirds

The Stoning of St. Stephen

I am not an apostle,
never the bearer of teaching, light.

Why then,
must the wrath of lapidation,
Jerusalem's Jew-fury,
be tossed at my kneeled pleading
like mad-dog turtle doves?

Jesus lived.

These stones are not cast by any soul
without sin.

Israel, this holy city, is gravid with widows.

True. There is not room in the theatres, temples
for all of their suffering.

But there is ample arena in Christ's heart.

That is what I told these black-born women.
This is why I must die.

Like Mary, many sojourned from the desert.
Like the dismissed beloved, there was no room in market inn.

This grifted gravel builds makeshift walls.

Witness of these pigeon-priests
pales to the altitude illuminating from my homing heaven.

The stones make a chastened grave,
not one shard liable for the requisite, lithic kill.

The Son of Man lived.

He lives within me, my sling masons—still.

Saint Christopher

Because your heart is an indefatigable explorer,
the wheeling mind and obedient feet must follow
its pulsing voyage-desire.

This is where I come in.

Mammoth as the Matterhorn,
more in tow than Captain Cook,
I have a history of carrying travelers—

to the other side.

With the Christ-child braced on my shoulders,
I bear a backdrop for lifting the weight of our world.

Burden me with sails to steer, roads to navigate.

Treading softly, we disintegrate bedded granite around the globe.

Be a kind visitor whenever, wherever upon your arrival.

Greet each host with passage-gathered basket.

Stay long seldom.

Do no thank me for your safe admit,
for I cannot charter

your welcome.

Rebecca

A shelved book
perhaps is the best way
to mark Rebecca
in, otherwise, rash passing.

Every community possesses
one—whether by outright ownership
or on liberty loan.

du Maurier entitled a novel of such a woman,
tucked corpse on a castaway boat of dreams.
Hitchcock printed her wintering memory on celluloid,
set the good theater, all of Manderley in posthumous flames.

You could dress her in white among flutes of fancy.
Still, she sat in the widow's station
where the learned page princess would remind you:
your promises were due—two weeks from today.

Citizens meeting and leaving daily
with her dismissive stamps of approval,
obliging to story time, beaten by the sea—

Rebecca lived, it seems, in a House of Maxims
where hapless actions spoke louder
than a room replete with wallflowers and words,

minding to public services,
keeping her own private Mrs. Danvers at bay,

until one page-turning Saturday night,
check-out time adjourned.

Matchless

What light, what heat
sticks like friction
in hungry hair—
no match for Despair.

Old Amsterdam—

I stand before the hoary corpse
of the Little Match Girl,
hung holly, sad sulfur.

Breaths of despair,
my wet boots attend
in storybook wonder.

If only I had purchased
a fascicle of her wares,
No.

If only I had been sufficient wind
to avert strike, her father's fury,
No.

If only I were the fire
she could not
put out.

The Ragged Men in Ragged Clothes

At Eternity's Gate, Painting, Vincent Van Gogh

The ghosts of Van Gogh and the simple man
are one.

Voiceless vagabond hunched in a cottage corner,
meditated in grief, hands decaying
in the weary face of useless,
blue garments of wisdom.

What he has burned, offered for charred sustenance
this evening, collects in a humble, threadbare smoke
behind his coat of anguish, twilled supplications.

The wood in walled hearth, sticks of sorrow,
from sun's flower to sun's regret, flick and flow
as workaday water under a daily-bread bridge.

His chair is thatched straw, a moth-eaten cross
he must bear until, somehow, each vesper,
evening prayer reaches a holy, uncircumcised ear.

The planks beneath his boots of earth and soot
serve as a road, portal to eternity's gate,
if only the sorrowing old man would up and wake,
wave the bluing morsels and moods
from his blessed meal plate.

But the ghosts won't let go;
in sheer misery, they saturate, occupy.
They burn like searing pinwheels
from intestine to eye,
seizing paradise from the soul and the seer
blinded by his own wrenching, wretched appendages—
self-imposed bandages of despair
disrobing last light.

The Lord, landscape, and sky—
a witness trinity that can only sympathize
on what is otherwise—a splendid—starry, starry night.

Fascicle

Album cover, Led Zeppelin IV

If nothing else,
the old vagabond
is about to build
an order fitter than straw.

He has faulted a thousand paths,
learned the moral
of each stone page and story.

Too weary for bricks,
his weathered frame
burdens what it can.

Upon his stooped bone,
a fascicle of sticks
gathers and flames
like a tangled cauldron.

These are from seasoned woods,
fallen forests, faggot-rich trees.

He has disarmed all wicked posts.

In plain-brown wrappings,
his last labor is to escort
these transgressions
away from the pastoral world.

A derby shepherd of sorts,
his shadow and staff
mark where village-stock once thrived,
where only quest and question remain.

In his loosened coat pocket,
he carries the vade mecum of time.

He pauses—
tips at all angles to prepare
for his wrestling with angels
before descent to the grave,
or better yet,
ascent of the stairway.

The Residents of Rose Hill

Stones gather like harvested dust
along the buzz-bladed drifts,
meadow dunes of Rose Hill
where a sleeping citizenry
hone their souls—
death's dwelling for the rain-minded,
a community of another coming
for those who wake in faith,
honor in hope.

The red and pink peonies fatten here
each spring; earth-blood flows
through dashing bud-branches
beating measure, meditation
with a syncopated sermon wind.

A chickadee pops its purpose
on a small wooden cross
for the soldier dead, nods its
badge hood—flit of respect—
then flies toward the full trill ahead.

The attendant census is one of stillness,
sensitivity, magnificent memory,
waiting for its walking young to visit
in smile and prayer.

Overhead—

crafted names, sage proverbs, quiet sayings—
blazon language of the eternal-nest natives in marble town
who settle their restful lots for God.

He calls them home.

They call Him mayor.

Mist of Grace

Grace walks with me to greet each day
She moves in quiet precision
Grace offers light to suggest the way
She whispers my life's mission

Grace lends a hand when I must fall
She reminds me to stand up straight
Grace goes in peace when duty calls
She is early when hope is late

—for Marian

Trappistine Nuns and Caramels, Our Lady of the Mississippi Abbey

Within this box of assorted nuns,
I choose the creamy,
uncoated ones,
the kindest sweets
knelt in translucent wraps
who package themselves in prayer
and light-corn syrup saps.

I select the goodie-graces
that the Lord and FDA inspect—
who daily take ethereal exams,
then pass each strict and silent test.

I crave the penitent, saintly ones—
who fold their palms,
make sugar from sour—
who keep themselves for God
and hermit's hours.

I want the dulcet dames,
quiet as a napping tabby
who prowl their vespers
about the abbey—

the chosen hands
who craft afternoon candy
with the Creator's blessing
and inundating, sisterly loving—

to darkness with dieting; I will take one dozen.

All About Sister Jean

She arrived at my home for the big dance on Good Friday.
Well, at least, her bobble head dropped at front door.
I had given up good sense for Lent, paid handsomely
For this chipper chaplain to be my date for the Final Four.

I asked her to be the patron saint of my bachelor pad,
This priority-mail messenger who had me at first nod.
Her rambling rhythms shook like a habit-dangling rosary,
Springing back "Hail Mary" or perhaps a "Help us all, God."

Fasten your seatbelts—

I showed her the secular sights all Easter weekend—
My broken brackets, my broken ego, my broken-down car.
Bigger than Nova's Brunson, mo' important than Wolverine Wagner,
It was Jesus and Jean who were the bumpy night stars.

She's settled down for the off season now,
This light of my living heart and room.
Together, we're folding scouting sheets that look like wimples—
That's right, the shape of a big "W."

The Hierarchy of Angels

God, being universal, delegates discrete authority,
Establishes functional hierarchy among the strata of angels.
This is the business of blessed, winged things.
The Trinity,
Obsessed with Triumvirates,
Spawns Three Spheres:

Bearers of God's Thrones, Priests, and Ministers.
Each celestial Sphere limbs Three Orders:
*
BEARERS
Gabriel (the brass go-between) and Cherubim (singers beneath God's breath)
Dancers of the intellect for the Omniscient Mind

The Seraphim (celestial serpents)
Breathers of heaven's fire, the eternal, not infernal kind

The Thrones (mirrors of the Lord's justice)
Minders of the quake, unshaken by the raptures of being
*
PRIESTS
Dominions (Divine bureaucrats)
Integrators of the spiritual and material, governors of reality

Virtues (beams of dreams)
Keepers of spiritual truths and treasures, God's trove of priceless chattel

Powers (collectors of conscience, drummers of duty)
Mighty mentors to soldiers of Earth's inevitable dirt, battles
*
MINISTERS
Principalities (Weathered ones of our upper ether)
Guardians, good for all groups—cities, nations, all of God's creations

Archangels (Blessing the down four-pinned creatures)
Shepherds to speechless, humankind's ablest teachers

At last, Angels
Lowly angels, bone-specific, still we laud them on high
Each a crucial fix on cross guard, until we are permitted to walk civil streets of the sky

POEMS OF MOTHERHOOD

Dumbo's Mother

Overprotective as a Big Top
above three rings
of high jinx, pie-sky illusions, death-defied wires,
Mrs. Jumbo is the kind-hearted,
paragon of a good mother
upon naïve silver screen.

What does she not stone-hued sacrifice,
endure for her calf-kid, blue-moon-eyed Dumbo—
born with bat ears, mishap's flaps, bomb-
blown roses, protruding toward rudeness, ridicule,
shunned by the other pachyderms,
juggled by taunts—down right laughed at.

Her maternal instincts, guardian nature
mistaken as madness
among the peanut sweepers, carnival criers,
the massive martyr finds herself trunked
inside captivity's captivity—a circus prison,
abandoned animal-train car, shackled in tears
beneath any creature's dignity,
beneath helpless stars.

Separation is separation—
whether it is by roaring oceans
or a few iron bars.

It is her own waterworks' boy, fear-flying
who discovers her binge-crying—
mammoth and child, appendage extended—
each searching for comfort's caress,
using memory, sense of tusk-touch,
gifts of Mastodon-snorkel skins.

Reaching, reunited,
the boy whose wings are like an invisible trapeze,
and his grounded, trod mother
its wind.

Baby Mine

Jailed inside a carnival train car
with labels for spectators and curious clowns:
DANGER, KEEP OFF, MAD ELEPHANT—
Mrs. Jumbo has been sentenced by a 3-ring court
to live the rest of her swatters and sways
trunked away in misunderstood seclusion.

Cozy ain't the word for it.

Love, or perhaps the more accurate term,
abiding friendship finds its way
to this gray, pachyderm pack-away chamber.

Escorted there by a uniformed, dutiful mouse,
Dumbo finds comforting mother and music to his overgrown ears.

These Stonehenge-appenged creatures innately possess poor eyesight.
Height constraints alone prohibit calf and captured to see.
But the animal kingdom is a jungle of senses and hunch.
Thick-skinned theatrics lead way to discovery by touch.

Boy Dumbo relies on his frontal bin
to meander, explore through the iron bars,
find the heartsick act with pink hat, trapped within.

Mrs. Jumbo lifts the crying cargo, her bulbous orphan—
sings…*Tusk, Tusk*...which is elephant speak for
Baby mine, don't you cry—

swinging her son in outreach, snout cradle—

such a tender, poignant peanut

this mammoth lullaby.

Mama's Boy

He's a mama's boy—

The collective clique-tongues at sanctuary
whisper/speak between slingshot
scripture and sermon—
something dodged from *John*
in fresh *Testament,*
a word, a verse about casting the first stone.

Charred like a comeuppance martyr,
I take my hits. For years,
their quibbling eyes have barbequed
subdued, unjust spit.

I die here, every Sunday,
as if fallen on Sabbath's sword,
unable to marry—
much less manage
to cleft the umbilical cord.

Still, I hunger.
Here's a hunch.
At break beyond noon,
doily lady will take me out to lunch,
a one-horse restaurant,
sneering patty-melt or steaming rib-slab,
why, indulging Mom even picks up tip and tab!

This is the grand buffet I get, gracious hometown,
for each weekly hour of heaven,
what I earn for Saturday nights
with the womb who brought me into such world—
both of us watching Welk's rerun baton
bobbing on public television.

He's a mama's boy! A mama's boy!
Check his freeloading skivvies for print pansies!

A mama's boy! The better bass and tenors cry.

(There are worse things I could be.)

Jochebed

Drawn to this world to servant-lead,
share God's glory,
you, Moses, my son, will soon be drawn
from a great river.

I cannot keep you in birthright form,
but reserve you in a righted heart.

The edict of the Pharaoh is written
in ferocity and fear.

You must float before its predatory page
swallows you in waters of lawlessness.

Consider this, first exodus.

I lay the last of your blessed infancy
inside a cradle of plaited reeds.

It is the hushing child who rides, alive,
among the rushing Nile, its resident saw-toothed smiles.

Afoot, I will shadow your primitive navigation, bankside,
like a tracker blocked of true light.

May your eye on God never dim, Divine treasures within.

I have faith in the barren,
the rich want of an Egyptian's wombless purse.

When I hold you again, downstream,
the knowing will be inherent, between you and me.

I will call you, *sweet child*.

But you must cry out to me, *nurse*.

Whistler's Mother

Arrangement in Grey and Black, No. 1, 1871, London

I told my Jemie,
that I would not stand for this.

So, here his mother sits
in hourly deference to his daddles.

The arrangement of coal-and-cloud paint
on his boards makes for such a maudlin piece.

Yes, I suppose reticent sentiment is the pursuit
of this portrait—so my corner eye tells me.

Indeed, I've got the morbs on my face,
as instructed, restrained like a draught horse.

I keep my periphery skills a secret,
watching him collude with craft, such austere weather.

The boy's adroit—I'll give him that.
Notice how the hem of my dress resembles high tufts of a curtain.

Darkness seeks darkness here.
Severity in bleak blemishes of white is the guide.

I further depress in a pall over bentwood chair—
all for his aesthetic—trussed, humble hue.

If the intent is reverence, sanctity of motherhood,
dear son, to the public and your domestic dowager—

you've got some daubing to do.

Eve

In this leafing light,
        appetite takes us there—
morning has done nothing
        but mold us into creatures
of ravenous bone. The ser-
        pent wraps itself around each hour

of my body, rubs
        language like lemon skins upon
my ribs and tongue.
        Around my flesh-belt—
I bear minimum wage,
        a child, all blue murmurs must nurture

until the most truculent of ages.
        A craven sun tucks
behind, beneath this tree of life.
        We are blinded into streaks—
of diminished reason, tempered by succulent rage.
        This is open-page omen

to remainder of days. The auditioning clouds—
        as formless as our intent.
This is God's hunger. It is his clapping consent.
        Oh, Adam, our throats dangle
in minstrel deference to His wooden, crossed strings.
        Gather oracle cores for Him,

pretend they are roses.
        Upon exodus for two,
perhaps we should stoop for bowing cause.
        It's bound to be the beginning of
a Good Book after the Fall.
        I can hear joyous thunder, what wrathful applause—

Regarding the Master Painters, Madonna and Child

Blame it on the blue distances,
the requisite deep bruise shrouds
that prevent, somehow cloud
all uses of canvass,
oil on wood, to portray
any appropriate
maternal-to-miracle gaze
of view unanimity, mode acceptance.

Raphael, Bellini, Botticelli, da Vinci—
select High Renaissance pick—
something quails
in each artist's depiction of her frail,
porcelain façade,
as if she is both virgin-stranger,
old-song swaddler to some man-child, god.

The positioned pears and landscapes
before and beyond immaculate hands
seem more like artifice, intrusion,
fruits and acres to re-create
sin and symbol, chaos, confusion.
Still, she holds the weltering weight,
bled to birth, framed and embossed.
Between flush horizon, specious vertices—
brush illusion to a cross.

Virgin Mary at Grotto of the Redemption with Baby Jesus

Here, in this castle, this cave of antimony and jewel,
the Virgin Mary awaits, salvation in arms.

Man of all men,
Stone of all stone.

Let us enter, you and I, for that is what humans do—
they go in.

Here, press this quartz, hardened query in your palm
as we search the lapidary's palace, blind as we are, press and bleed.

Never has darkness known such light—
never descent afforded such lift.

Strip of garments, wear only the water pressing your eye.
Strip of all secular thought. Let prayer, redeeming wonder, amass your mind.

Here are the grottoes, such monumental tithes.
Prowl with me, alley creature, among Jesus' nine lives.

There, in cavern of choice, Mary ascends between ruby and sapphire,
above Purgatory's redolent ways, desecration, Satan's bluest fire.

Wed to heaven and earth, naked devotion her ring,
she gestures us to dig for an underground spring.

Here, friend, accept Father Dobberstein's trowel—
deeper and deeper—at last, healing Higher Ground.

Look up and look out—what vision more miraculous than this—
as if we were with Bernadette of Lourdes, sighing Ava Maria's first kiss.

The babe cradled in pearl of her bosom—appears—
the Immaculate leads us to the cross' last station, Carrara stone tomb.

Here, she redeems us, silence rises, ecumenical tongue—
with no need to say—for Death did not enter that mournful day—

Who here among you, killed my son?

Resurrection of the Widow's Son from Nain

Altar panel by German Renaissance painter, Lucas Cranach the Younger, Luke 7: 7-11

Black-hooded, draped in splays
of somber grief,
these people of Nain
traipse upon the stone pathway
from synagogue to end-gates of the city,
tolling in silence—for the departed, beloved
like a procession,
a peal of mute bells.

At lead of the lamented,
a widow arrives to wit and journey's end,
kneels before her dead son's bier
beneath an empty slate sky,
dry silver chalice.

In the distant range from grit mist,
gears and grains of hushed, ruinous day
push and wheel as they may.

The Lord's compassion enters
this realm of sorrow,
touches the sleeve of widowed, bereaved.

All weeping ceases; all wheeling stays.

The still son rises from his coffin
to face the order-hand of Our Savior.

Remains resurrect—a miracle among the meek—
once humbled, resigned.

Over the ringing tongues of Galilee and Judea
the silver chalice spills luminous wine.

The Madonna Was Yours for Free

You have been paid for—

These were the words most resonant
with me during Maya Angelou's inaugural poem,
On the Pulse of Morning, for President Clinton.

And I thought about my boundless ancestors
working for pennies, laboring for nothing,
how each of their couplings and connections
must have been necessary, genealogically exact
for me to be.

We children were not born with tweed schemes on our backs,
wallets to compensate the delivery nurse and OB-GYN
as infant seats trekked us away in tufts of pink or blue
to awaiting stuffed creatures zoo'd in freshly painted rooms.

Oh, we cried through the cords, contractions
of placental descent,
but we did not know it was pain—
because our bundling emotions had yet
to experience first joy.

That inaugural exaltation happened,
still happens,
when our soft spots and swollen noggins
are brought face-to-face
with the colossal virtue, virginal woman
stranger smiling at our helplessness,
beloved birth mother—
bracing our craniums and spines
for the demands, delights of this life.

She, miraculous harbor, is comfort and wing,
clearing the caul of our confusion,
breathing us into being,
this daughter of the Holy Madonna,
loveliest of light
our earth-worn eyes will ever see—
she who pulsed harder than labor—
and did it for free.

—for Rachel

Rose of Sharon

All dust-drive long,
I minded and coddled
my unborn child
with wishful ideas, self-pity,
and preoccupied prayer.

I was all pick-of-the-peach dreams,
tending to California comfort,
mother-in-waiting, secretive things
about to be brought forth
from the fertile valleys
of that fruited state—
and furrowed within me.

The grapes hung in the west
from a shooted vine
of Divine distance—I trusted.

Nothing, no weeded corruption
banked upon our tumble wheels
stalled my troth in immaculate fruition.

Now, upon golden arrival,
I fall, an abandoned ma'am crying
over mother's milk unspilled, unused—
baby-barren, my drunkard husband,
high-tailed like a runaway deer—
leaving a family of one.

In this whispering barn,
it is as if winds of the red country,
gray country have trailed me here,
mocking my ignorance, giving last tufts of air
to suffocating delusion.

All that remains is my bloated bosom,
deflated cradle of a crushed goddess' urn—
and a rib-reckoned man—yonder
suckling starvation in the crook of a corner.

I hoist my reckoned, robbed body—
walk a field of faith toward him,
offer my loosened breasts to the crack of his lips.
We are pacified in bruised exchange of *hush-now* concern.

Mother Goose at Fejervary Park Children's Zoon, Davenport

Next time you're there, tipping into the petting zoo,
notice her paralyzed presence among runaway leaves.

She is shocked the children, the characters she groomed,
would take their pies, sheep, spiders, and horns—leave her to grief.

Those wired spectacles cannot make-believe her mind.
She gave her young legend, climax, happy endings, shoes.

Still, it sounds to her—their contrary goodbyes, quite unkind.
With time on down feathers, what else is an empty nest to do?

The passageway through her breast, to her heart, is cupboard bare.
Her white frame bumps at goose thought of kids who visit-enter.

Blue as the flop-hat that tops her statuesque air,
Mother Goose parks and pines in shade of everyday winter.

Left wing of longing, right of recluse—in granny tandem,
nothing but rhyme on her hands to nurse her through hurt of abandon.

Fairy Godmother

A bibbed matinee kid once said
between cheeky, chipmunk stuffs of popcorn,
slurps of straw-drawn fizz cola,
I looked like a blueberry muffin with a sparkler.

He should talk.

Sweet as I may seem—
This is no easy occupation, cozy calling.

These kingdoms come with their limits.
The feudalists are faithless;
their men come with catches and chinks.
It takes more than a tinkering with a bell.

True, the pumpkin as carriage was an indubitable work of art.
The rest, as one might guess, is all Bibbidi-bobbidi-boo—
brimstone, frolic-freckles, stardust shampoo.

Cry in the bucket corner. Tap your shoes.
Who am I? What do I do?

Dressed like a monk moored inside a blue curtain,
caped cathedral—
I am mentor, co-conspirator, embodiment of hope, friend.

But try telling that to unappeasable princess after princess,
pity-pool girls, seeking a horseman, footman, and charming hand.
And then there are the dowdy ones, cinder kept,
cellar wept, who haven't a glass chance of tumbling upon the throne—
but their humble tongues request it—nevertheless.

It is time to take the confections from the stone oven—
or else the moral will overcook, burn to crisp.

All we need to ice these dreams to satisfaction
is someone evil in the lass' bloodline, or step-bloodline.

And wand-walah! The candy-coated conflict is ours to win.

-for Dora, my spirit board rival & friend

A Lady Tremaine on the Family Tree

A wicked aunt once spritz-ly told my charming mother
she was a nobody who came from nothing.

My father's snobbish sister,
her tongue—fat-ass,
broken foot-glass—
sure was slather, pumpkin-rump something.

The her-to-her heat was some argument
over how the other fallow but fertile girls
treated Auntie's own willowy-wimp daughter.

Hierarchy speaks, cinder to peak.

Concerning my nin-poop kin's soft offspring,

I believe

the fries-with-that world

got her.

Halfway Home

Home Semi-Sweet Home

I step in; I step out
The arc-apex of middle-space is halfway home
I am measured by the distance covered
Front leg first & heel to toe

I move in; I move out
The wheeling cargo is halfway home
I choose the path of most resistance
The miles gone are miles to go

I am in & I am out
This passing fancy is halfway home
I am treaded by the vehicle of trend
Driven by those paving the road

I reach in; I reach out
Free hand in the kitchen jar; I'm halfway home
I take only what occupied time allows me
Clearing the shelf-gardens honest digs have grown

I walk in to first, then head out for third
Second base is halfway home
I want more that kisses from this diamond mound
A virgin-jewel thief on the prowl & probe

I breathe in; I breathe out
One last exhale; I'm halfway home
I have lived to be the death of me
Tripping over light, I fall on stone

Charley Horse

He was a mean mother
of male molecules of sorts,
that uncle of mine,
that Charley Horse.

Spasms, this nephew has'ms…
if my Mama tells me proper
how he trot-treated the schoolgirl
during the better-her-than-me
depression break-my-ass glass of the 30s.

Riding eat-my-dust high
each penniless sunrise
to rural school,
ignoring her dehydrated cries,
enough room in the saddle,
but not enough grace
in his dry-fly heart,
to offer her a-stride,
push the little girl off,
force baby sister
to gait in pain—

Is there a forgiving twitch
in her lingering calf,
nervous as it is,
to excuse his cramp ass,
to make requisite bell
before its rendering
tardying shrill?

My mother—
she survived this cruel leash.
She survived to read this.

She survived that corpse hog-horse.

She survives him still.

Dust Bowl Girl

The Nancy Hanks rag doll
dragging lines at a lag-angle behind her—is better off.

Well-clothed, composed, in fitted paisley scarf and snug boots,
the limp figure is sewn and sealed—from hunger, longing, and dust.

As for this rewrite of a girl, revised daughter
in tatters and cinder—
she passes famished pumpkins
on explained way
to a one-room school
where, upon arrival,
she must focus-knock
for quick entrance to bar
the whirling drafts of soil and soot.

She dutifully sits
at a two-seated desk
bound by a thesis about best heads, caste-iron frame,
branded by inkwells, hinges, and proven grooves.

After trace-pledge to a browning flag,
her voice is all numbers
in rhythm, accordance
to teacher's arithmetic stick.

Then a break, for winded breath
before a lesson in letters,
the stories of stellars
her favorites—and she dreams
between syllables
of becoming a great author
if given a crash of a chance.

Come mid-morning recession, the hopscotch hour,
she'll skip and pick up plum seeds
then trip in laughing quota of despair
over false hope and stones—

such portentous grapes of wrath.

Poor, Pitiful Pearl

Named for a concealed gem,
hardened by desperate times,
in the assembly-line ocean of toys,
she is hooked and lured
by icons of Poverty and Concern
to live the rest of her days
as a peculiar doll on Earth.

An anachronism to those
who have gone trinket-fishing in boom 50s,
her tawdry orange hair, irregular face,
more fit for Great Decline of blue 30s.
Poor, Pitiful Pearl is out of place
in the aisle and age of first Barbies,
even within the discount bin—ordinary disgrace.

And on her sullied hem,
a scarlet patch, not unlike Hester Prynne,
who can match Pearl's disbelief to the letter,
for it is not little girls, little girls who buy
this would-be-retail reject
too impoverished to wear a costume disguise—
no, not little girls, but grown women
who through their purchased furs, fat purses remember—

when nothing in the kitchen stewed,
FDR announced entry in World War II,
and not even a stocking or whiskered tree stirred
in their pale houses of bleakest Decembers.

My Poor Mother Worked the Mines

If the truth be told from those dark tunnels,
it was my father who literally was the coal miner—
holding his own, beyond the angle of repose
in destitute shafts of Appanoose County,
speaking in canary-story about his collects,
his conquests—to strange patrons
in barstool aftermath.

But I, the youngest child of four,
prefer to believe in my mother's work,
her own mines she endured
before my eyes, in stoney-end metaphor.

The barrier rocks of time she woke to,
the stratum bed, the break lines of
sweat and surrender she offered
each day, to keep us children fed.

The light she clung to
when all dross, dust and dreams
had long abandoned.

The floor she provided
when structure gave way
to pitfalls and gaps.

The intake of air
her lungs sacrificed
so our own mechanisms
knew nothing of want, the meaning of lapse.

My own mother worked local mines in immeasurable lift,

never earning a shine of a wage—
but the pressing company kept her to the seventh age.

My mother remains a pillar,
though the coal drifts are gone,

And, woman, you punch-perfected one helluva shift.

It's My House

Come to my porch, Breath-of-Suffer,
resuscitate near death, this desire—
the loss, not of losing,
but letting go.

The silver leaf chilled
knows the white dust on the branch
bears the long tooth of winter.
Lovely, how lovely, the rooted grow old.

In the cellar, dank stupor,
sealed fruits of the forsaken—
Hands of Lament let the rope
to the Underworld's core.

Come, Breath-for-Another.
To desire is to suffer.
The knock is not hard
until you open the door.

The Accountant of Hours

She makes in the diversified light of morning,
the motion, sounds of negotiable birdsong—
such are the capital exchanges of the stay-at-home mom.
How discordant the scrapes of breakfast, the balance sheet of her day become.

Nothing aligns in the rooms of this woman's domain,
errant balls-and-jacks, outgoing clumps of fine hair,
incoming paper airplane attacks, cries and complaints
breaking like ocean swells, dulcified by the offering of peel-away snacks.

She herself does diddly with her winks, so society thinks.
Stereotypes gather on teeming green lawn like weekly ads, wet papers—
Mass consumer of bonbons, addict to soaps, neighborhood drama—
She's good for going for groceries, easy errands—that stay-at-home mama.

Her ledgers are otherwise empty, this bringer of babies.
To her credit, he'll keep her, logged as a domestic asset—
a couched colleague who examines, computes, ensures, inspects.
She certifies his raise-worthy rise like taxes and death.

Die Mutter

Mothers of the Holocaust
concentrate on the newborn,
unborn, still born, descendants
of Jude, cast in yellow swaddle,
bearing the unorthodox star,
the sacked maternal ones
who cannot lift, bear industry
weight, those who have delivered
nothing but faces of naïve fear
upon a regime's stone plate.

Where shall their dark coats congregate?
Where shall muted lungs speak?
So near the hissing visitations,
enervating the angered weak.

To know the sun is to become the White Rose,
belief in leaflets;
even in uneven Europe,
a righteous left wind blows.

Who would harm a tracting teat?
Who would hurt any German girl?
Who would malice the infirmed
echoing a captive's cough?
Who would turn the gas vans
at Ravensbruck chambers either on or off—
at mirror command of mere Adolf?

If the answer is not to be silent,
perhaps the offer is to pray,
diplomatic detainment,
amputated enhancement,

halo smoke—from far away.

Anne Frank of the Attic

This is not the world I wanted,
a kind of sinister, simmering endurance
where the brush of a kitten
or tap of a porcelain cup
summons instant seizure,
eventual death.

I can change letters, sentences,
thoughts, whole pages,
but I cannot transform the war.

My mother is near me,
but I am far from her arms.

My family and the huddled others
lives as a sort of one-celled creature,
unified fear, programmed effect,
confined to the cause of the Party.

We lie about the attic like trunks of old clothes.

I come here, not to the annex,
but to you, Diary, for refuge and sanctuary,
your bindings attuned,
open to original hope.

As routine as the hours are practiced and pass,
the atmosphere breaks each daylight, in silence,
to a disheartening divide.

Beyond the bookshelf downstairs,
there is a hissing.

I surmise it is either a tea kettle or a spy.

A Partial Colossus

After Emma Lazarus' THE NEW COLOSSUS

Titanic was to consort with my torch,
bring to me her tiered wealthy, pugnacious poor,
heralded masses from the celebrated sea,
not these numbed-and-stunned fractions,
blue-hinged refugees, numbered survivors,
one for every two deceased,
without pride, without purse,
continental refuse of Poseidon's curse.

Beneath my heft of liberty,
they still appear homeless, tempest-tossed,
cataclysmically incomplete to me.

It is not nice to beguile the Mother of Exiles.
Grieved, I crack the light on this forlorn golden door.
My gift, my lamp moves along the paralytic shore.

Sagittarius

I should not speak of stars,
much less shoot at them—
but what use is my aim,
if not to raise these arms,
this string and frame
to both intimidate,
honor the skies?

I am halved
by the universe,
part heel, part hoof,
planted upon terrain,
yet raised beyond roof,
an off-color balance
that exists due to advent,
ballast of wintering blues.

Those stars,
they taunt this centaur.
I'd murder their stellar arrests,
if only I could
manifest what my pose
toward the cloven
clouds suggests.

I am both god and fraud—
why not? It fits.

Archer of dormant anguish, awake!

I release this wishing, watering head
of sapphire stone
toward the Northern Cross.

It hits

into a bluing bewilderment,
the sleepy, estranged
in loose firmament
will know
as slaughtering,
swaddling swan and home.

Hinged Wood of Holiday Good

We could call it a Christmas box, yuletide coffer—
something that holds, durable remain.
Epistles sound like ministers.
Let's keep its contents as letters—to a drift-away child.
Gather round its diminutive monument like a tree skirt,
learn the message these passages, this melody contains.
It spins a rhetorical riddle
resonating question
What was the first gift of Christmas—
a refrain that roasts like a kernel on open-fire.
Rest ye gentle the riddle—
Love as an answer seems too broad as a blue star in a far field.
Only pensive shepherds can claim
the initial offering was a child,
the seasonal wraps in the name of Jesus;
but from the Son of Man, Son of God's swaddle,
perhaps we should consider another—
the nodding bow and lift of cerulean, shawled grace—
the love of Mary
or any mother.

Some Children See Her

Some children see her as buddy in ringing home room
With sugar-shape cookies for holiday buds to consume
Some children see her as buddy in their home room
With ladle of fruited punch in a cup to boot

Some children see her in wispy front yard
Buttoned in golden red coat like a Christmas card
Some children see her in wispy front yard
With leaves cradling on snuggle-me snowshoes

Some children see her with rain-cane in hand
To offer a roof from dip clouds' command
Some children see her with rain-cane in hand
To keep those slipper-soles shiny and scratch-new

Some children see her pup-paddling at mom-and-tot
Wearing a one-piece cupcake suit that good sense forgot
Some children see her paddling at mom-and-tot
Sinking and rising among the kid-giggles of summer blues

Some children see themselves dished in her arms
Swaddled near her breast, blessed from a world of harm
Some children see themselves dished in her arms
A dove with nothing but love to coo

The children of my hometown
They know her pudding face
And light with spirit
With her cuddling grace
The children of my hometown
They know her pudding face
She treats each
As if brought to this place
With a silver spoon

Fruitcake Weather

A flock of gray goose-feather clouds
hover leaf-lotted yard,
brink of balding woods.

A threadbare woman
rises from her wrinkles
to iron out the day.

Fern frost climbs
the single-pane window
like a crystal arachnid.

It's *fruitcake* weather.

She speaks to her tea,
then saunters to the pantry for inventory.

She will need—her particulars

ingredients—listed like sleigh reindeer

a dash of rum, a dance of whiskey
prance of black currants, sapped cranberries
cube of candied citron, blitz of all-purpose flour
Maharashtra mangos by the minute,
Savannah pecans by the hour

the red noses of bing cherries.

The cups and spoons have not abandoned her
like the dead clocks on the wall.

A stone stove lights coals on cue
to make the merry, madcap of it all.

Marjorie's May Baskets

The nimbler, more fragile
her finger bones become—
the quainter, more appealing
the may baskets.

Each cuddled bushel
of candies, snack grains, and leftover
Easter bunny grass
huddles inside a diminutive wedge cup,
pleated pucks, the kind you rinse and spit in,
at the dentist after a good cleaning.

And, indeed, it is a good cleaning
my mother wishes to celebrate,
like a trumpet, resplendent tendencies
propounding soft weather's triumph
with fine friends, each peach-of-a-spring
she lives to honor in gratitude
the pink stiffs and yellow reaches
casting their coordinates
among lush tufts of green.

These happy hampers
of lilt, edible fresh laundry,
cut from cardboard, but woven
with scissors-skill and craft care. Individual
as a snowflake, caloric, yet, lighter
than air.

Her sobriquet for these clarion bouquets
is a nut cup.

I imagine her tiptoeing to a house step,
perhaps hoping for a catch and a kiss,
knocking briefly before dismissing
herself to a humble, safe source.

My heart hangs there for her—
much like those kind, floral weaves
on a neighboring door.

Tea Time with My Sisters

A Foreshadowing

Not a cup of bliss,
scarcely a saucer of glee,
tea time with my two sisters,
one indelicate afternoon—
a hemisphere and several ages away
from Victorian London.

Our play cardboard table
propped in the living room,
dimestore kettle, stale sugar cubes, steeping leaves
aligned among the plastic
pink etiquette of service,
guest doll of choice
to fill the void of fourth side, empty chair.

On oldest sister—Susan's cue—
Mom pressed the 8mm's
polyester fraying black button,
instigating the Sirius-like bulb
to bark blindness in our dining eyes.

This was apropos moment
for the bully of the house, Big Brother,
to enter the forthcoming fray with his shoe braces,
storm the affair, doff the doily cloth like a bad magician,
wreck the service of proper protocol—
Susan's quick resistance, retaliation
of whacking him incessantly with guest doll of honor
captured for time-of-your-life memory
with Mom's disbelieving eyes, rolling film.

Little sister Carol was a far cry from assistance,
steamed and bawling to a scarlet simmer.

And I, I draped my head with the say-cheese tablecloth,
a Hollywood shawl, my Nora Desmond fifteen seconds,
stared deep into the bright eyes of the dark show box,
taking the just broken limb of the flinging doll
in my arms like a trophy, thanking the Academy for this honor,
then singing a few chanteuse bars of Peggy Lee's
Is That All There Is?

Staying Home From Church

Take what you want but leave the rest…

We didn't feel much guilt,
we household kids on Tenth Street
when the folks let us stay home from long sermons
those short, wintry Sundays.

Dad would start his cough and car
by mid-morning, drive to Rita's coffee shop
to pick up a sack of caked sugar doughnuts
that looked like battered boulders,
so greasy and good
their sweet sweat made the bag
translucent—permitting hymnal light
to glisten from the precipitating paper.
Shoveling the choker holes toward us
at the bin of binge eating,
the work-wrenched man
fed our compliant tongues like spring calves.

No, not much guilt—in fact, more like a gathering
on our terms, my hungering siblings and I,
full and content in the basement,
Big Brother now pacing like a soldier-priest
in front of the foot bed, ministering a lecture
from the High Heavens to us three unwise youngers,
nodding like manger stock to holy stricture,
the dung on his chore boots draped with more faith
than those windy-den, bedroom fumes.

And there was always, time,
tenacious time for a home-cooked offering,
a ceremonial omen of sorts
when his grub-hand would take a souvenir plate
from a Silver Dollar City, family two-day vacation,
take that plate and pass it around
to my sisters and me,
insisting we pay our coined debts
to rid our sins, keep our murmuring
hearts whole.

Staying Home From Church

Yes, there he stood and spoke,
a handout with a treat-tote for his own,
our grand brother and stand-in savior,
pilfering sense from our innocent pockets,
nickels from starved socks,
trust from our souls.

—for Susan and Carol

Rockford Sock Mittens

The poorest girls seem to possess the richest memories.

Take my mother, for instance—
she had all the demographics
stacked against her
like a tall drift of blizzard against the barn:

The Great Depression,
small-town folk in southern Iowa,
one-room schoolhouse,
single pair of shoes for the winter,
single pair of mittens for life.

She lost those hand warmers,
somewhere between number-fingering and flirting;
retail replacement was out of the question.

Like FDR, her mother made her a New Deal:

a second pair cut
from Dad's work-worn Rockford socks—
freckled gray, red-nosed at the heel,
snow-capped around the calf.
The feet were worn out, but tops were still good.

The footwear was molded into finger furnaces, overnight.

How proud she was to show them, even to the snooty girls,
their pleated noses boarding the pulsing bus.

Shouldn't the poor girl be saddened by the privileged laughs—
shouldn't little Marjorie hide the makeshift footings
from the nettlesome mocks that leave a heart in need of darning?

Why, no! replied her discovery eyes.
Upon my palms, I can feel my father farming.

Babes in Basins

When her children were young, she bathed them in tiny basins,
cleansing their concerns, anointing the scrapes of another day at play—
water from her palm pouring onto sensitive skins, the touch of her hand,
a visionary guide, prompting drowsy heads to bed, the dreams of beyond.

As her four tadpoles outgrew the confines of these bubbly bowls,
Helen showed them the rivers (she knew she had swimmers)
where they could wash and wade on their own. Mom had thrown out
the bathwater, but never withdrew her love. The children always knew
they could freestyle back home.

When she knew she was dying, Helen gathered new basins,
though her children were cleaning kids of their own. She filled the baby pools
by clipping and collecting moments from their days of first paddle kicks,
waves of wonder, arms up and through. Keep your head above the waterline
when the invisible currents shift from down under—trinkets, tidbits, and flashes
to nurture their memories once her course was run.

This is a kind of lifeguarding itself—after the body vanishes—
keeping the souls of survivors buoyant—afloat with treasures, no doubt,
these basins hold. A photograph can hold its breath longer than the most
seasoned diver. A fraying yo-yo returns to the spirit like a floating ring—
returns and returns to the grasp of an awaiting finger-fold of old.
Helen left no long letters to explain her departure. She always trusted the water.
The sea of stuff filling the basins was the merry time, maritime story she told.

—for the Jerry & Helen Hampton family

Black-Eyed Susan

My feet have never broken the soil of India
My eyes are not native descendants of Amerigo Vespucci
I am the daughter of an unknown tribal man
Generically classified as an Indian,
Politically refined as a Native American
I am the surviving member of a vanished clan

Black-Eyed Susan was my name
Though I could not keep it
I was born along the Trail of Tears
Like the wind
My father rose only to die
I buried the rhythm by his side
Where it has remained dormant
For one-hundred years

Without my father
Denied my mother
I left the badlands of Oklahoma
For the banks of a northern shore
A white trader from Missouri claimed me
The voices of my conscience blamed me
As Black-Eyed Susan became Susan Eleanor

That was the last I saw of the wind and the rhythm
As I entered a world so foreign and dark
I played the role of society's captive
To mirror the shadows seizing my wild heart
And it was my heart's own remorse
Running like a team of untamed horses
Striding in vain to catch a whisper
Of my family's faded cry
Unable to keep pace
Absorbed by some holy human
Susan Eleanor lay Black-Eyed Susan down to die

Black-Eyed Susan

Now, I am an old woman returning
A century out of style
Capitalism and computers
Concrete stretches
Where my unscathed spirit once roamed for miles

The call of confusion abounds
As the language is awkwardly passed around
From one acceptable term to another
Drawing blood from my veins
The Bureau of Indian Affairs attempts to legalize
Something no Awareness Month will ever realize
I was your sister, and now I am your brother

When my ancestral flesh-and-blood discovered
A sepia-ghost photograph of me last summer
Those ancient rhythms revived to dance
The orphaned wind caressed my sleep past evening
I close my eyes and dream of the chance
Of wandering down to the banks of the forgotten river
Leaving my civilized clothes on the shore
I immerse the souls of Susan Eleanor and John
And emerge as Black-Eyed Susan once more

Alongside the gentle clap of waters,
A legacy of lost people awaits to embrace me
As we speak in silent tongues
We are old in nothing but wisdom
The untouched world around us is young

My feet have never broken the soil of India
My eyes are not native descendants to Amerigo Vespucci
I am the daughter of an unknown tribal man

-paternal grandmother of poet's family

The Robin That Stayed for Winter

In the backyard roams a single bird,
        A kind of migrant left behind,

Rust-breasted, searching for his sort,
        While bare weather gathers high.

He does not November swim and, thus, missed the boat.
        The late worm anchored his duty, no doubt.

His round of fellows flew in sudden coup
        To roost and rendezvous due south.

A lantern lass spies him there from frail pier-porch.
        She muses in wonder his precarious isolation.

Despite spring-sign's widened eyes, quite walnut-sized,
        Her concern turns to the sparse of things—privation.

She will offer seed for his nimble needs,
        Toss wreathed berries when laggard wing sings for supper's favor.

Each to each, through diminished days, beak and beacon will keep
        Good company and good neighbors.

She's Gone to the Birds

Birdseed roosts
at the perch of her grocery list.

These gleaning, pluck days,
the noble woman speaks in two dialects—
grandma and birdsong.

Morning congregation,
earthly migrations,
Gaia's answered prayer—
the watercolor wings—
collide, reside there,
fishing for worry-free worms
and sunlight—
doting to signs
of weather's fitful, flighty ways.

Plume and brood
gather in search
in trust
of her happy, indigo mood.

Reliant as plum-fetching robins, come sunrise,
friendly as impulse's smile,
their frigid feathers collect
in groups for which ornithologists know—
a raft, a siege, a colony,
a parliament, a parcel, a gaggle
a charm—they are hers.

She enshrines them in portraits,
porcelain-shrine monuments;
the fine lady entrusts
their embodiments,
fixated flocks in her living room.

Even when grounded, soiled,
nest-drenched in cold locks of April rain,
these molted messengers sing
to her soul—ever upward, skyward

unhinged and undisturbed.

The Mother of Trees

God refused to fit her in evergreen fir,
so she slips on the ice for winter kills—
haggard branches, egg-empty,
rock-candy coated, gossamer gloved,
nesting nothing but wicked debris.

Bereaved, her hanging glass
crosses the wires, detours the streets.
Chaos and crystal in freeze-frame,
she leans.

Her children long left her,
seeking fleeting careers in bags of leaves.
Her husband, faithless as summer;
nothing, but hard wind, to solicit as lover.

Snow blind from overtime—
spineless spring,
the mother of trees
heavies as she blows,
bereft in clinging beauty,
foreboding pose.

She crackles like a hidden witch,
bends her broom over pitch roof,

and breaks the stone house

where a once beloved family

once trusted her roots.

Winks

My mother's aging
is a kind of sleeping,
an act of beauty,
princess winks.

No prince
charming the object-world
moves her.

No hand mirror,
laced in pearls
catches what
her shell-slumber reflects.

She is deep and deepens,
waving safely past Earth's
bad apples, black-hooded queens.

The wicked, pirate hour
about her herring-bone frame
chooses wisely
to forsake her.

My mother's aging
is a kind of sleeping.

And in the happy end,
only a kiss from God
(in cape and tights)
will truly wake her.

POEMS OF UNLIKELIHOODS

A Certain Ambiguity of Spring

Spring begins its wee creep—
or is it that Persephone
rises from winter fires
to the beckoning blooms
of home?

In this season of source infancy,
the gatherings of encroaching crocus,
assorted advent of green,
one cannot help but wonder
if there ever was a world
of loss—
the memory of churl-winds,
Demeter's moaning grief
across the picked fields.

Why then,
do we stand before
this just-fallen man,
a friend to births and breezes;
why must we, again, mourn
beneath a lily-strewn cross?

And the trees,
they dress, they put on
for the warmer tilts and term
after stripping
their crowns clean
for the cold stare of a wolf moon.

Perhaps there is nothing more moving
than the cessation of breath
upon a blue daffodil's request—
this infernal, terrestrial
tug-of-war, perpetual storm-fest
between half-husband Hades,
and one akin to Mother Nature
who pines half-the-year's course
for her harvested daughter—reclaimed, removed.

—for the Ralph & Billie Evans family

Petrichor

There is a coming word for it—
the stone-fluid smell of fresh, foreboding rain
after a dry spell or weak winter.

This blue umbrella of bliss-weather
about to shake,
spill the spring beans.

All the air one's nairs can consume,
hangs in damp suspense,
waiting to burst its ambrosial bouquet.

If only my long-stemmed love were with me—
to travel gladly among
such private flowers.

Pluvial, some scholars may note it—
but the romantics search further
to capture a phrase for its ghostly command.

The outdoor room is a hint of perfume—
with neither blossom nor bloom
in sense or sight.

Such a windfall perplexity, olfactory pleasantry
only the great freight of nature could create
with such small hands.

Ariel

based on Shakespeare's THE TEMPEST

Synonym for trick,
imprisoned by a
disappointed witch,

you the obedient
sprite who defers
to magic hands

seizing a mostly
unmanned, underhanded
island,

I suppose I
could ride you
from both bookends;

as one, we wonder-grow
from pirate isolation
faith of symmetry, friends—

winged with empathy,
pursed in goods,
tendering evil to

legible moods, like
flying seahorses themselves,
spine-plated, all shifts and sails;

yes, we airborne elves
we melt
into one blue delude,

brooding, breaking wall,
be both
framer and defect

for due course,
a fool's déjà vu
in memory of—or tribute to

inevitable shipwreck.

Twenty-First Century Grief

It is brief
like a tweet,
transmits its gray face
through cyberspace,
born, I suppose,
in the down dust of island towers.

Friended by insincerity,
comforted by fake news, caffeine,
it cheats *clean* inside its own handkerchief,
cries like a cued crocodile to the pied drumming.
It reads *Revelation,* pretends to know
the last book got it Rosebud right.
It looks back, at happier runs perhaps,
but still sees the wheel-fire coming.

Accidents

Who cannot help but turn,
stare in wonder, amazement
at the slip, mishap, broken-plate bruise,
whisper that better-him-than-me
self-assurance under the breath—
the nodding, knowing rubberneck.

Why, it is as if each passenger
by blue interstate is a gaping tourist,
each crash-course,
concave design per vehicle
a canyon
with cloud pity
sailing over sobering, fluid steam.

Both parties exchange cards,
contact numbers
as if picking up hookers.

Admit nothing
except it happened in a flash
like the end of an affair,
or invitation to dream.

Sorrow in the Sycamores

The Verona dead, too, are concerned
about a boy in the trees,
gray-gammed, blue-moon sleeved,
in sorrow, it seems, about an Artemis gate,
ovaries his passions cannot open.

His spoiled boots,
not among those bloodied,
mischievous heels
in servitude's civil fray.
The little lord's mother, Lady Montague,
sighs in relief, prelude to eternal grief,
at Benvolio's reassurance,
her unrequited son sobs—paces away.

Send in the clown—
infernal invitation—
mottled by errand,
otherwise, creamy-white,
illiterate, ignorant
of clarity's tragic,
forthcoming torch
pinwheel of poisons,
quick-drug delights.

Meanwhile, the aphid boy,
like his select grove of lifeless limbs
appears sick, more
feeding a frenzy of misery,
dolor-confessed, Downward
from this market of mayhem—
summer's exiled leaf drifts.

He murmurs absurdity's certain thought.

An abiding sun rises.

The folly earth shifts.

Hardships

These are the sails most unenduring,
or shall I say, enduring;
for what choice possesses
my garden of sea grains
but to harbor their beaten bows
as they lap to bitter-breast shore;
and something abides within each hull,
or perhaps in my heart,
something rhythmic, salt-storied,
bearded in blue, anchored in black,
something like waves
surging forth—from a disturbed god's court,
these nautilus-shroud soldiers,
for whom the common islanders cry, *fear*
and know by no other name
than the ritual tide
of untimely setbacks.

Shanty Town

The town is a wretched stretch of trains
with broken wheels berthed on wrong-winded tracks.

A station of routine lament, abandonment—
horizon choked by bleak quota smoke
of clinging industry that, when gone—won't be whistling back.

The poor are passengers here,
plentiful as snowflakes, bunched to fall
on their sooted boots and dreams.

Why, it's Christmastime! Who conducts this chaos?
Will Santa come with painted toys and tables-a-plenty
to engineer and skirt starving-child anxiety?

Do reindeer alight and pause upon roofs
crafted from fruit boxes, walls of crude wire?
Will the sleigh give way to makeshift stays,
crash into the hub of flawed cardboard desire?

This town with eyes of secondhand coal, transient souls,
hitched to uproot-me caboose—

Oh, will Santa come to such a heave-ho, hum-drum
when its indigent citizens, too, are just passing through?

Paper Ghosts

Once she is able to speak,
Ann vows to collect paper ghosts
in lieu of paper dolls.

Her articulate hands will craft them from images
of sepia-toned photographs, and she will hang some
like branch-torn paratroopers along invisible halls.

They will play open-heart house,
savor vaporous tea,
these fragile frames, thinly-linked, but strangely secure.

In time,
Ann will give these wraiths delicate wings,
but never firm feet…for they must never march off to war.

The Kiss

V-J Day in Times Square, Photograph, 1945

If only the aftermath of war

were to remain like this,

the dame embraced, a soldier kissed,

her pointed heel

in ecstatic pirouette,

when a war hero's lips

takes her purse of passion's nets,

her spine in suspended recline,

elegantly bent like a swan's neck,

whirlwind minds entwined.

If she were made of strings,

he'd pull from her clinging waist,

send her spinning

among the scatter-fly ticker-tape.

If only this steam would never simmer,

this frame forever freeze

to capture this rapture

this flood of overjoy

that can only arrive

with service from overseas.

American Duty

She is always
under the roses,
beneath the bed
where earth's bed
is wine.
What is here—
horizons deny me,
vertigo abides me,
the axis scents
of sex & sky.
This grasp of lattice
on behalf of lover,
between chaste lacework,
thorns of Twenty,
Descent, I climb;
for she is always
under the roses.
Pause—but
do not bring her.
Inhale hereafter.
(possess time)

Auditioning for Monet's Garden

Welcome to Giverny, you budding aspirants!
A flower's papers must be in order.
The resume'—water tight—with a reflective quality.
Patience is a requisite outside the high stone wall.
Naturally, both Monet the man and artist must favor you.
Now, let's see—can you work in spring or do you prefer autumn?
Don't fuss with a card or sack of seedlings.
If Claude wants to hear from you, we'll call.

Are you familiar with triangulation?
Color, perspective, and symmetry—
How you petal your wares against others?
Any allergies to flora, ecstasy, or fame?
The Garden speaks in languages Japanese and French. Do you?
Could you promptly learn upon brush appointment?

Quickly, I need plants A through M to follow me—
Aubretias to magnolia daisies.
Come, fleet-of-leaf, as instructed into the Clos Normand.
We will further divide upon brute inspection—
The arid from the aquatic, recherche' from the common.
Azaleas and lilies, continue immediately to the basin-pond.

I must ask you all to remain silent as sage uncertainty.
Shoo away, you shutter bugs!
No photographs beyond this point.
After all, all lasting impressions will be made by Monet.
When he appears with his palette, gaze into his façade for count of three.
Then dig deeply into the sod.
Oh, by the way, never, ever call him Claude.
Au revoir and shams of four-leaf clover!
A tip from one who has stilled for his practice-portrait—
The secret is not how well you look in pink roughcast tones,
But before the eyes of God.

Bohemian

I am here; I am there. Place is not my own.
I scatter cinders, crumb-memory of birds, remnant dreams.
By sheer movement, one's fixed nature is known.

Old step is such a giving stair, then a stone,
leaving me to hold the cold candle, out-out frayed seams
unwinding—I am here; I am there. Place is not my own.

I must've been a poet once whose verse turned to bone,
set in a pot of water simmering belly-up schemes.
By sheer failure, one's wicked nature is known.

Then a philosopher, no, a painter brushing upon privation's throne.
And set to music, yes, rambling music, silver and keen
staccato-noting…I am here; I am there. Place is not my own.

Excuses, stay mobile within me, make the rent, shifting home.
We'll know consumption by the lung, our only means
to justify further waxed venture into dubious unknown.

These roots are brief, seed-sparse—nothing reaped, nothing redeemed.
Verge of question remains to mention: what is the edge—if not extreme?
I am here; I am there. Place is not my own.
By sheer movement, one's fixed nature is known.

Flow of Thought

I sink or sail along the current Perception
Mystic brew, clear-blue, color of the sea
Filling my mind-matter with the hope of liquidity
Downwind of absolute lucidity
The promise of a grand river passing
Through the backyard of my foreground
So roll, roll on, Perception
Spill your ethereal wine
Pour the overflow into my thirsting eyes anew
And bathe in the cleansing of your most astute waters
Your stream of unconsciousness whirling into my waking conscience

Titanic Doll

Porcelain should make one dispassionate,
a manufactured actress
who does not wet or feel—
removed from the pulse of playtime—
not some raggedy refugee
who blinks, with the ship, goodnight.

I have lost her,   the girl.

I know her only by touch;
never trust a doll's eyes.

Muted by misery, this Sunday sleep's mutiny,
how can I call out for her hands?

There are nothing but hands all around me—
flapping and flinching like flensed seals.

I do not want a mermaid nurse-mommy.

I am not impressed by this marine arena,
Neptune's playhouse.

I am dressed for story time and prefer the predictable ending.

I miss her spoiled pout.
What must be current   is washing away—
the smile painted between my cheeks.

The sea is a shell.
I can hear home in my ears.

I will require no further changing.

And I do not need this ocean to be soaking in tears.

Isidor and Ida Straus

It is said *Titanic* can travel up to 24 knots.
We, Isidor and Ida Straus, prefer to travel as one knot.

Those are not lifeboats entering the sea,
but floating devices descending to separate the inseparable.

The iceberg, indeed, is a blue-veined mistress,
splitting up the ship from its tattered passengers—

but she only interlaces our lives, hand-overhand,
to sure harbor, steadfast land.

What travel is this,
to embrace and accept our voyage to the eternal world.

Infernal, icy waters enter the deck as dagger-fountains,
ripping and wrenching all formal and informal ties.

A moment's disaster cannot unbind
these 40 years of Macy's fame, fortune—the feast of family.

Charitable strings of the orchestra
play our song of love and lament.

Had we been richer or poorer,
there was never an hour more nobly spent.

We are dying together, more tightly, closely
than the clench of any cold could ever entomb—

soul slipping into soul, bodies bent.
Death is dessert, and here, here—lie in waiting

two perfect
silver spoons.

Rhymes with Ocean

All of love is motion,
And the only movement here—
The manufactured waves
Of the tragic monolith,
Descending from the vested sacrifices
It required
To trap in its passion, its quest
For the cold ocean bedding.
At last, at rest—
How moving the stillness,
Lovely, this absence of remorse,
As if deep travel, indeed, removes memory
Of the heightened fury
Our aboveboard world will not soon be forgetting.

Provender

Pilgrims of the prairie,
each with a girth of three ships,
the livestock gather with bowed skulls,
ruminate their lumbering prayers
before the founding rock of grain tables.

Their voyage is one of storage.

It is a christened calling of the blessed corn-fed
to crack the yielded berries, partake of the by-the-bushel bird,
treat themselves to the time-share trough.

Farmer Profit looks over horns of plenty—
        feeding off the fat-Atlantic of the land—
                to become gravid fat of the land.

Beneath the heft of hooves,
November's plain spreads its ocean-cloth of amber waves.

A majesty of purple mountains to the west
overlooks the fodder-feast and reigns as lot-tombs of lavender.

In town, the butcher behind chilled glass awaits, the after-graze
with white wraps of surrender.

Amidst the silo's warrant storm,
fattened cattle are froth and forthcoming. Yes, the cattle are coming—yonder.

Profit-misers,
inspect, look at their Plymouth snouts,
cumbersome wanderings amidst the beef industry's tricks,
thrash-waving tongues—lapping the salted-licked trails

of provender.

Among the Brome of Autumn

Among the brome of autumn,
I down my wintry home,
Beak to spur, my trench unstirred
A few hours from first snow.

A cocked gun swells, sport of smell
I've heard declare before.
Hunter routes German pointer,
A theater for war.

Old World birds fill scenery.
Endangered, my allies,
Speak to me, so quietly,
Of death-stalk in the sky.

The grouse is a bit mottled,
But he cannot complain.
Bobwhite on look-out's tell-wire
Warns of All Saints' shell-rain.

Gestapo spots his rooster.
My brood stills as if unborn.
I alight from grace and fright
Above the standing corn.

The gauge is at the ready.
Season tolls to doom's boom-sound.
I fall to earth, gauge my worth,
Oh, captor, of high ground.

Hunter, leave me dignity.
Remove not my red mask.
Waste not my feral being.
This is all I ask.

Among the Brome of Autumn

Cold marksman's blade, resting shade,
Flense my warm breast apart.
Give to me clean dignity.
I, pheasant, give my heart.

The partridge sings to free me,
But I am more than free.
Celebrate on caroled plate.
I wing to fruited tree.

Among the brome of autumn,
I down my wintry home,
Beak to spur, my trench unstirred
A few hours from first snow.

Mindful Winter

I feel I possess it—a mind for winter,
what with this face full of coal
to counterbalance
a midsize ball of ice for a soul.

Cognizant of cold—
top-hat regard for both Frost and bough,
I reflect in the bow shines of silver,
withstand what makes the weathered vane bray.

I, too, bear down
from the hoarfrost on leaves,
mint and mingle with begotten, bereaved,
eschew all flora except the whitest of flowers,
stir the season in spoons and sauces of dark, endless hours.

My true temperament short as daylight,
the carrot on my nose,
I wait in a façade of fluff-flurry
to grip with lake-effect snow.

Grounded as an impudent child,
puddle-packed with little to lift, inspire
save these terse sticks of makeshift
walk-on-air wings,

I hold as the Old Man himself,
pulling on down—the nothing that is our own—
among such diminished strings.

The Balloons of Macy's Thanksgiving Day Parade

They are their own kind of miracle
affectations of invention, putting on airs
helium-heading toward 34th Street and the flagship store
with marching clowns, high school bands, live animals undertow.

Braised in disbelief,
we sit in childhood wonderment,
table bird in the oven, cup of egg nog in hand,
ourselves—bus tickets away from the kick-can-cans of Broadway.

Hoisted by handlers, above lamp and pavement,

these lofts, these behemoths of the streets
they lighten each leaf-fallen soul,
a sort of aerial train,
string car after string car—
caricatures and characters of popular culture—
sponges, superheroes, cupcakes, caped dogs.

We fasten ourselves to their fascination,
hold fast to the imagination
trying to let itself a-float, loose.

This, that is all engineered
by the century steam of a department store
with St. Nicholas at the caboose.

As on a Wintry Plain

The ghosts won't haunt, still you lift a ride,
take a team of eight by gossamer reins,
colorless journey, save the chestnut sleigh,
through barest of birches, no limbs to hide,
except your sparse bones in their waning lives,
to scarve you or scar you, whatever pain
that will encourage the ghosts to mush again,
slant eyes of white wolves running in full stride.

What keeps you, child, on such long, wintry plain—
the blush ahead is not one of summer;
it is last regret, a light in faint fog,
to give you false wish, a fool's wonder.

The ghosts break for last bits of prairie grain,
then forward lift toward the face of God.

The Fondness of Summer

A Song for Edie, An Early Practice in Alliteration

Here in the summertime of the year
When the boys swing from the trees
The sleepy swimming hole bursts into a wall of waves
As children chase baseballs and their dreams

There came a lively lass to our tired town
A bouquet of beauty to all bearers of T-bats and balls
When she sent a smile your way, you'd swear on your starter glove
You were face-to-face with a breathing Barbie doll

We lads would leap from those lofty limbs
Scurry to North Park to give our boyhood luck a whirl
And fight with flying fists for best bleacher seats
To gather a glimpse of our golden girl

The Junes and Julys seemed to rise each day
From the locks of her sun-kissed hair
As she strolled through fairways and rolling hills
Footsteps of an angel forever imprinted there

She moved like the wind of an August night
Eyes encompassed the reach of oceans blue
To this tiny town trapped between two cornfields
She brought the beaches of Malibu

The ageless trees still speak of a tender time
When Jeremiah was a bullfrog, and the levee was dry
But the boys have left the leaves of those obliging oaks
Ball caps in the attic make way for suits and ties

The laws of nature, the will of God
To these, our folding lemonade stands and lust must endure
Brother, steal a base or a late September kiss
Alas, she will be absent from the autumn of our lives

The summer belongs to her

A Lady for Small Occasion

Better than a man of grand season,
bequeath me a lady for small occasion,
the night in, with popcorn and Bing,
a walk with our low-rider dachshund,
a rocking eve, home-fire doors
shut to champagne avalanches
this bubbly, intoxicating, cumbersome world—
my own private confetti who never forgets
she first was gift's girl,
a damsel in a state of landslide undress,
a *willinger* who never says *no*—
unless yes is out of the evening's
influence, nevertheless,
a party girl who solely thrives
on a pint of winking ice cream
topped with a blush of toy fruit,
a beauty who thinks lovely is overrated,
but nothing is more underrated
than cute.

Thanks for prom—

The Death of John Lennon

We were under the ping-pong table,
putting backspin or topspin
on our restless adolescence,
when one of us overheard from Howard Cosell, of all people,
that John Lennon had been shot.
Yes, Monday Night Football was on loud volume,
so no one could hear our lobbing under that tight-strung net.

You sat up in your layers of crushed blue-velvet robes—
strategically placed between your sophomore breasts
and my junior desire—like drifts of deterrent snow.

You were crying gently and then spoke of Yoko Ono
as if you knew the famous Asian, fresh widow
—or your dad once made melody with her—or both.

I retorted Ms. Lennon looked like she should be working for a camera company,
and only wore sunglasses to shield from the tell-all world
that the woman had no talent.

I'll give you this.

You had purchased the duo's *Double Fantasy* disc over Thanksgiving weekend,
the only person I know who did not acquire the kiss-kiss cover posthumously.

I suppose that was when I realized—name dropper that you were—
perhaps you were a bit revolutionary, or a revolver, whichever fits a spinning gun.

We taxied back to Lennon's death throughout December and winter break
like a plain clothes stalker in Manhattan—arguing, one-upping
each another with tidbits of Beatle trivia and bookstore memorabilia.

By Christmas, you had given me enough Beatlemania clippings and conversation
to fill a yellow submarine—paparazzi shots of polarized-shaded superstars,
among lonely-heart throbs of fans—both of us lying
about reading *The Catcher in the Rye*—or understanding Mark David Chapman.

One of us signed both of our names to the *White Album*,
then spent a lifetime being Communist, blasphemous, wrenchingly unclean
between fretboard shifts and mid-bridge career spasms.

We could've made beautiful weeping guitars together, kid—can you only imagine—

A Silver Bell for Pamela Powers

It was Christmas Eve, 1968, a Tuesday.
My big siblings were home
from a coal-grueling semester at school.
Our eyes were glued
to the gray screens of living-room tubes,
not waiting for a letter from Santa—
but a blessed message from the Moon.

Apollo 8 had reached lunar orbit;
the three astronauts on board—
Frank Borman, James Lovell, and William Anders,
like three kings, delivered passages from *Genesis*,
photographs of glorious earthrise,
and visions of lunar mauve sugarplums
dancing in our hero-hungry heads.

Every five-year-old child in Iowa like me wanted to be
an astronaut for Christmas—
By Eve's end, we all wanted to be detectives.

An unforgettable, disbelieving blizzard of tragedy happened—
not in space, but here on earth.

Someone, a ten-year-old girl from Urbandale, had been abducted
from a YMCA in Des Moines on the day before the holiest day.

Somehow, the local television stations posted
what looked like a school picture of Pamela Powers all day long—
in a corner of the frame, during festive programming.
She looked like anybody's sister, anyone's child.

Pamela had asked her parents to stop at a pet store
to hold the animals, comfort the caged paws and purrs
that had not been selected as lively gifts for the holidays—
before attending her brother's wrestling tournament downtown.

At the meet, the girl wanted a concession treat.
First, she must wash her hands.

Pamela Kay was never seen alive again.

A Silver Bell for Pamela Powers

We Iowans did not know that, of course.
Hope hung like unspeakable wreaths among us—
through Christmas Eve and Christmas Day
with no sign of Pamela, nothing to report, but to keep looking.

My mother spent most of that yuletide time
weeping over oyster stew and potato soup in the kitchen.

Like I said, I was five—
I kept thinking Santa Claus or God would find her.
Weren't they everywhere, able to see everyone and everything?
One of them could rescue Pamela and deliver her for Christmas.
I believed.

And what about those three wise guys floating around the moon—
If they were true crusaders, couldn't their mission be changed
to save Pamela Powers?

Three astronauts, Santa, and God—five in the sky
Pamela Powers would be found.

She was found alright,
but not among the busy sidewalks, city sidewalks of Des Moines.

No. Pamela's body was found in a ditch near Mitchellville, east of the city.
She wore nothing but a blanket of Christmas snow.

I knew of the Grinch, the abominable snowman, even the wicked magician—
but I did not know evil…until the day after Christmas 1968.

Perhaps there is nothing for the town crier to ring,
not a word to announce—
except pangs of empathy, care, and grief.

Bless the down child,
bless the surviving children of Iowa, Christmas Eve 1968
who would've exchanged huling hoops, crying dolls, and dreams come true
for her safe return from a momentary visit to an unimaginable moon.

The Starling Flew for Days

In America circa 1890,

a Hotspur lover of Shakespeare plays,
released these European black-bard wings—
some devotee of Desdemona,
fan of Caliban, deferent to Tybalt.

Yes, a New Yorker, if memory clears,
engineered rebel-romantic scheme
to propagate the iridescent piers
to disembark from Central Park.

They fled. They bred.
Too many adapted. Too few flapped dead.

Most damned and defiled in apocalyptic flocks,
derailing airline engines,
plaguing anguish over soil and stalk.

Is this the British liberty gift,
or some disastrous act of torch retribution,
reparation for giving the flag and finger
to Our mother shore?

The oft livid, loud-lingered shrieks
sustain to flit-fancy over both plain and peak,
shrilling heart-to-hilltop
Mortimer! Mortimer!

Ah! The clamorous ring
like a hot-tempered tambourine!
(Don't these displaced beaks know
that we the States are the weathered, newborn king?)

Whatever the ill or well—
at least, we won the War.

Katniss

Resourceful shoot, I, too,
live off the earth,
hunting and gathering
parcels from the sun.

Upon release,
each passing winter,
I defy the scars of weather
and stirring beasts.

My green arrows
long for the grasses—
these blood-tinted petals
open to move.

Here come the quickened children
in winner-take-all fashion,
seizing another spring,
killing for a score.

I have faith in my crest,
these garden markings,
surviving each trod invasion,
perennial affliction.

A cluster of wholesome old folk
gather at the streaked window
with apocalyptic hands,
motioning the primed tiny monsters

for more.

Miss Havisham of the Meadows

After Dickens' GREAT EXPECTATIONS

This is the release I wanted—
the decaying mansion, the stillborn marriage—
at last, both institutions set me free.

Nothing in Satis House has satisfied.
Even the cliché fog of London lifts
like the hand of a porter accepting a continental pass.

A new woman needs a new world,
the meadows of America,
rising as fine stalk to face a sun-dripped prospect—
in lieu of the marshes unsteadying the past.

But, Pip, the damned wedding gown—
                                        follows me here—

the fluff-fuzz of an early dandelion,
                the veils of white violets,
                        a skein of prairie clover.

I wear them as the soil wears in the wind.

Between two rivers, I see that I am only between tears.

Nothing here has moved beyond heartbreak.

Again, I am left at the tattered altar of my soul—
explaining to a dark minister the great flat lands—

I have come to expect.

What If We Spoke

About our vices,
gave each other
a good ice chewing,
paper thrashing,
rings of rectitude
finished in
crab-summer smoke?

What if we splayed
in tongues the bodies
our collective codpieces
wished or went
ahead laid?

Wouldn't be neato
to confess without
duress all we rolled,
carded, levered,
and lost—
in the discarded
family casino?

What if we made
not love, but sound—
in wilderness harmony
with rib-worn hounds—
what it's all about
in this doubtful town....

Because It Can't Stop Now

That's why it's still happening,
will continue to happen.
Too many of the jig's pieces
either won't fit—or are too affixed.
It's about gun rights and gun wrongs—
our helpless accompaniment
to play along.

I can walk into any school
I want to.
I can bring any tool.
After all, I was backstage bullied;
The front page will tell you
I was bruised.

I don't make mark;
I can't rate grade.
I mock at sports
I've never played.

My dad owns weapons
he thinks he's got
locked away.

You've got too many doors,
not enough sensors or guards.
The morning announcements—
fish in a barrel.

I've never hunted game in season—
but this isn't hard.

Haven't I surmounted the deaths
of 9/11? Brought you to your "never again" knees?

It will take airport, airtight
homeland security
to protect your children

from a one-time, combat child
like me.

To Throw a Bone

What if this is nothing more
than to throw a bone—
to pacify, pitch an idiom,
flesh-gesture, appease,
placate by means of shell-remedy,
healing, nonetheless,
in its faint spring breath
to restore
as time lengthens in April season
but, nevertheless, shortens by
in a grander scheme,
sure-dogged demise,
to the eventual stone silence
where all secular,
godless schemes ossify.

Cold Moon

December 3 and 4, 2017

What is this flawless light?
Utopian monocle—
I should know it,
without glowing inquiry,
without weaponry charge.

The crowning pearl moves
somehow within me
without ostentation,
requisite card.

I look for hanging metaphor—
bagged potato,
harvest lard.

It has no atmosphere,
only white-flag fury,
imperceptible degrees of disguised fire,
infinite measures of palpable ice.

Waning as a crescent.
gibbous as an ass,
whatever's perfectly clever
in myths of leave blue—

contrived, construed—

this beautiful cruel,

too, shall pool and pass.

Kitchen Sink

Death of poet Sylvia Plath, 1963

I wake
& dress
in raiments
of *Winter Trees.*

At last,
Morning Song
lip-synchs
a dirge ironic.

The oven door,
Daddy's visage,
It will do.
It will do.

The pipe,
his tongue.
The gas gives him
b r e a t h.

I inhale.
He slips on
my head,
this old black shoe.

Fellowstone

Most of my Old Faithfuls are gone geysers
by now. How I steadied myself
among the sediment storms and rim,
careful to oblige—never to fall in.

They were wise kettles indeed—
withholding, yet hot-spring honest
in each interval spill, timely and tenacious,
renaissance revivalists, if you will.

The heating cooled, plumbing kaput—
each chamber sleeps in ageless ease.
Nothing erupts; the pressure's off.
An onward flow, magma-mum's the word.
Lincoln Park is soft; no ash aloft.
All is urned and undisturbed.

—for Kent & Clay & Mary & Gretchen & Alan

Frost Heaves

In her wintering intuition,
a swelling solution—
or disgraced dissolution
as if the pumpkin-fresh crest
of certainty were about to break.

All has fallen of autumn, trail end of sled season,
dark-twisted pathways, embittered vines.

All honor has been his—
harvested, given to fresher claims.

Layers of fine-grained suspicion
wrap around
her ex-blithe, simmering, scaled soul
like a hissing scarf.

Beneath her evergreen veneer,
the burgeoning lense is ice clear;
a clean skate, alas, edges to a knowing coil.

Spring—with its purple sprigs, finch wings—settles in,
an uplifting, only to provide fuel to the shame.

A veil of valiance, defiance heaves like a raised brow,
bursts through society's innocent surface, scandalous plows.

Its unforgiving mist forges, disfigures atop such susceptible soil.

Turncoats of March wither in renegade, traitorous splays—
granite-feathered and marred.

Summer is a three-pronged throng of rises and sets away.

Still, it is scarred.

Loon

Across misty-dyed waters,
the common loon
coordinates a gray call
to relocate
its suited lost mate,
both arrived in the same,
yet unfamiliar place.

Marco Polo commences
between crested plots,
enchanted *echo—long—echo*
over, above, throughout
crazy lake.

Abreast strangers upon touchstone surface,
a decree of distance,
a cavern of ultrasound, canyon-captive aches—
ripple-wither rhythm,
sonorous exhale of blues—

—the agile arc of impulse muse-tuning
that hithers—me to you.

Some 38 Minutes Ago

Friday, November 22, 1963

Death, the news of it,
the broad break of its cast,
took its own bittersweet time
in the have-a-dream hour
of 1963.

Rude interruption of As the World Turns,
the world waits…

A welling Cronkite, in tears, black and white,
reappears some half-hour later, to confirm
tragedy in Texas.

Television executives scrambling
like encryption pixels on screen
to gather the latest cornucopia of copy—
live video, film, still photos—
traveling over wood and river
to national headquarters—

The newsman on the beat, on foot, in Dallas
too slow on the draw—

America in abeyance, on hold, midday moratorium,
grating its gums, bleeding at heart and teeth—

Is it ambiguity, ambivalence
or blind-flight ambition
circling its wagons
in shape of the Oval Office—
what with Camelot Majesty assassinated,
Red Button Chief killed?

The deep freeze, deeper finality—we the people feel
when Time both passes like a state funeral
and marches still.

Untouchable

Beware the storefront of my smile
The façade on my face
Legions of lesions and lovers
Hidden in place
A face full of promises swept away in the past
As I descend the pearl fittings from heaven
To join the ranks of an ascribed lower caste

The millennium has mistreated me for so long
The century has cheated me so wrong
As if I were born

Untouchable

Withdrawn in shame and silence
A soul shattered apart
My fingers reach down among the ruins
To strangle my heart
A face full of promises
Once basking in light
Masked by the Black Plague who seduced me one night

The millennium has mistreated me for so long
The century has cheated me so wrong
As if I were born

Untouchable

I am a harvest-moon flower in autumn's chilling hour
My leper-like leaves are untouchable

I am the thunder of meekness, wonder of weakness
My bludgeoned spirit believes this
I need no passing prayers, no lullabies good night
I need the miracle cure of love
To restore the morning of my life
Oh, how I feel this

A harvest-moon flower, autumn's chilling hour
Leper-like leaves

Untouchable

Breaking but Not Broken

If you leave first
for some comfort on a cloud,
an angel-hair atrium
offering no cratering return,
I will walk the unfair earth
breaking beneath my feet,
breaking but not broken.

I will attempt to speak
among my siblings and sorrows
wrenching words twisting
to make sense of your retreat,
my voice breaking
above the soul's resolute defeat,
breaking but not broken.

The sun will port my heart,
exposing rues and heavy hues,
along its high chariot street,
dropping beaten runs each evening
where the ruined and sundered cleave,
collecting our chambers, quiet angers
like charitable coins, drumming us to sleep

in rhythms breaking, but not broken.

Sadness Is a Place

We learn it as an abstract noun
Intangible to the pupil's optimism
Below see-level
An *–ity,* an *–ism*, a *–tude*
A vapor reduced to tears

But Sadness is a pace
I have correspondence of despondence
With its town-and-country face
A miasmic city-state of sorrow
Floating through a deaf sound

Its great, gray smokestacks
Emit monoxide anti-smells
Noxious, noisome
To tickle the passengers in air-tight garage
Too melancholy to complain or cry

Yes, Sadness is a place
You must slow down
To keep up pace
A tourist distraction
Visited by those unafraid of water
With tickets to sigh

Apria

Apria should be the name
of a Greek goddess
whose pulchritude lives by a brook,
not the calling card
of an oxygen-delivery company
that leaves a family breathless
when the lungs are unable
to blacken any deeper,
when the deductible has been met;
but assurance pays no more.

Enter, Apria,
for my father has died.
Grace your loveliness
over this house of mourning-pearl interim.
Extend your winged appendages
to collect these tubes, tanks, and belts—
this hospital bed on loan.
Abscond this hardware, my dad's second skin,
from the weathered eyes
of our overcast home.

Then away with you, Apria.
Ascend to your waters
glistening with fresh stone light,
resplendent like a prairie star,
for the strike that has darkened
on this swollen ground,
where because he has been,
we simply are.

—for Clifford Paul Thompson

The Respired

Breathing lessons have expired, sound the knell
Death enters the classroom and tweaks your nose
In time, you lose the scent but not the smell

The lungs are last to quit and push to swell
The air that you breathe at semester's close
Breathing lessons have expired, sound the knell

Oxygen gone, students exit pell-mell
Their huddled bouquet reeks the tone of sorrow
In time, you lose the scent but not the smell

So, why respire when the throat's afire? Hell,
You'll never learn what the Instructor knows
Breathing lessons have expired sound the knell

The aroma of darkness absorbs cells
You've earned the course credit now pay off the loan
In time, you lose the scent but not the smell

We sniff what the metaphysical sells
Then suffocate beneath trivial stones
Breathing lessons have expired, sound the knell
In time, you lose the scent but not the smell

A Grain of Salt

cum grano salis

You can take this world with the grains it gives you—
the good sail of a good harvest,
a weeping heart when the reaping is sparse.

Bitter and sweet are from the same recipe,
each to each with its own pinch.

In the ocean of things,
an iceberg is but a bit of freshwater salt,
essential to animal life
in its smallest of quantities.

But this boat is about to take an overboard overdose.

The chlorides of collide ominously appear.
All reverent form a circle prayer
to make the sting in the steerage less severe.

The less reverent throw the corpse that is colder
over a blue shoulder.

The soup of sorrow is on.
Wrap any leftover lifeboats up in aluminum swans.

Dignity

Transcendent of beauty—dignity,
this inward leaning,
inherent knowing,
civil parent to oneself,
womb of modest,
self-reliant love, a
Thoreau undertow without
stark disobedience, argument,
pompous resume' or grade,
a quiet corner of
sustenance, succor,
deep-lying, beyond legend—
a home base,
found quest of value,
the fetterless soul
handsomes and favors—
nevertheless.

Up!

We'll go—
perhaps in
different shifts,
in time,
on cue
to random
blue mist.

Up!

We'll go—
in tan-
dem trust,
deep sigh,
fresh hue,
fade to
soft bliss.

Up!

We'll go—
truant from
rules of earth,
its brute schools,
whiplash lessons,
our best guesses
will no longer miss.

Up!

We'll go—
cirrus-fleeced
children, balloon-born
for the Sevens,
clouded in comfort,
healed by helium's
delirious lift.

The Snow Geese

The snow geese
precipitate the sky

with winter
wings

V-trekked,
beak direct,
any route but circumspect

a rage of horns resounding
across the one true open road

flurrious flock
insistent that fall yield
the right of way

their down drifts
across the dark lake
of frosted reeds,
& the last departing loon

autumn abandoned,
the gaggle rules,
accumulates in a solstice sky—
stark cornet's cry
announces in stentorian tune

He He
as as
we

comes again
& soon!

Vessels

If you believe in anything,
believe in vessels,
ships of the whisper,
boats of abundant blessings,
come-again cargo,
gifts from God's inexplicable sea.

Believe in the message of the bottle,
folded and tucked
inside the body of a blood-relative boy,
purpose and plan,
the wave and wand of His invisible hand—
the time and tides that carry you to me.

The Raking

Veterans' Day, 2017

She rakes to weep, and takes her weeping slow
November downs like a deciduous leaf
The collect of colors a kind of letting go

Nimble wind, it hints at sign of first snow
The air fills with good-byes; birds take green leave
She rakes to weep, and takes her weeping slow

Silver tines of memory filter and row
Brown grasses, fell loved ones, compartments of grief
The collect of dolor a kind of letting go

All is dry measure except tears in check and flow
A bushel of sorrow, peck of disbelief
She rakes to weep, and takes her weeping slow

Armistice weather gathers in clouds gray and low
Immobile as tombstones, bound in a blue sheaf
The collect of honor a kind of letting go

Bagged and tied, this blessed burden to tow
Winter taps her shoulder, commands its seat
She rakes to weep, and takes her weeping slow
The collect of colors a kind of letting go

The Summer of '42 Retires

Swift summer is blessed;
her hour knows.
She slims her skin
of winter's robes.

Her moons are brief;
the sun breathes long,
smooths the scales
of Pisces' song.

From spring ides
her rise, an aqua bloom—
petals of heather steal me
to her summer room.

June's fire flies
& August hides
to skirt the heat—
July's entwine.

The autumn flowers;
September leaves.
Our solstice love suits itself
in shawls of listless, linen memories.

An earth-tone vest,
one of us dressed
for fall.

Because He Lives

Song of Resurrection,
Song of My Mother,
Song of Ourselves,
Song of All Souls—

This is where affirmation meets
confirmation in lyric spirit
of the cross.

A living Christ keeps my mother company
in glowing confidence.

Why, she perks up like pipsqueak in the pew
every time the piano bars begin—
God sent His son….

Palpable the music in present tense,
assurance of glory, riveting celebration.

A part of the Holy,
she is daughter, dutiful sailor—
navigating the truly future,
its righteous and wayward river.

An empty grave has filled her heart—
it loves, heals, and forgives.

My mother's choice hymn is a blessed jury;
her voice lifts in accordance
to pronounce the joyous verdict, valiant justification

Because He Lives.

The Remnant Garden

Impetuous to question—
but what will remain,
mere paper bags and plums—
once the nursery maid
sings her last sow-note
to the garden?

Will the rake be lain
like the *Dresden Venus,*
merging with rolling hills,
deliverance of repose,
coined in a landscape
of quiet silver?

How will the stones align,
born weeds be tended;
what reach will rein in lottery leaves,
soften the bereaved;
whose hand will deal lot and land
like a seasoned mercer?

Who will raise, palliate
the complaints of her children—
left to faithless fury,
their headstrong ways,
bowed at the lone trowel,
bending no further?

Dahlias in December

Not even the snow pillows accumulating,
comforting the sky
can appease these briery stem-wreaths.

Why, it is as if
their skirted red lifts
serve as bookmarks on the pale lawn
stiff reminders—
circulation of season
the loan of summer, shelved return of winter.

And there is a plum-worn woman
at pose window, Maria—
mulching each decade,
reading the street as if she were perusing
a favorite magazine,
keeping time, her steadfast mind
with the passing news of strange cars.

Her margined heart has been repaired
by trained hands and hooks;
it longs—all afternoon long—
for the bloom of a visitor.

The pinnate partners on the landscape,
dahlias in misfit-isle distress,
remind her of interval pills, needling labors.

A sudden austerity overtakes her gaze.
The dignity of duty, soft pangs of the hour
begin to harden.

Alas, the silver-tubed bell, has its cold-breasted way.
But the blood-hooded habits remain.

There will still be a garden.

ABOUT THE AUTHOR

John David Thompson is the author of 12 books of poetry, including E*ast of Eden, West of Astor Street: Poems of the Andrew Cunanan Killing Spree; Titanic: A Centenarian Voyage in Verse; 99 Voices, 99 Lives: County Poems of Iowa* and *Iowa: A Place to Poem.* A lifelong resident of the state, Thompson holds advanced degrees from the University of Iowa and an MFA in Creative Writing/Poetry from New England College. Thompson's poems have been published in the *Harvard Review* and the *Des Moines Register* among other venues. A United States Senate Scholar and member of American MENSA, the poet has completed post-graduate work at the Harvard Creative Writing Program and University of Iowa Writers' Workshop, both with honors. Thompson lives and teaches at the college and high school level in the Pella area. His third, upcoming book on Iowa will commemorate Iowa's 175th birthday and is scheduled to be released in 2020. The poet may be reached at the following email:

iowapoems175@yahoo.com.

Also, refer to Thompson's Iowa poetry at this below website.
iowapoems175.wixsite.com/mysite

NOTES ON SOME POEMS

Sonnet of the Angels-The poem is an acrostic verse, the first letter of each line representing the 14 offspring (4 children, 9 grandchildren, and 1 great grandchild) of Marjorie Thompson.

Rebecca-The poem is a dual allusion to the classic book by Daphne du Maurier made into a Hitchcock film and a hometown librarian who is very missed.

Dumbo's Mother-In 2008, TIME magazine named Dumbo's mother / Mrs. Jumbo the "best mother in pop culture history."

Rose of Sharon-character from John Steinbeck's THE GRAPES OF WRATH

A Lady Tremaine on the Family Tree-title a reference to the wicked stepmother in Cinderella.

Fruitcake Weather-inspired by a phrase in Truman Capote's "A Christmas Memory."

Sorrow in the Sycamores-from Act I of ROMEO & JULIET

Shanty Town-from a family favorite holiday tune sung by Eddy Arnold

Mindful Winter-inspired by the winter poetry of Wallace Stevens and Robert Frost

The Death of John Lennon-what I was doing the day Lennon died

The Starling Flew for Days-The title is from a line of ""Sara" by Stevie Nicks of Fleetwood Mac.

Frost Heaves-bursts of thawing soil in New England during the onset of spring, often causing breaks or concrete and general havoc

Some 38 Minutes Ago-phrase spoken by Walter Cronkite announcing the death of President John F. Kennedy in the early afternoon of November 22, 1963; I was one-month old, being rocked by my mother.

Dahlias in December-inspired by the annual dahlias exhibit at the Iowa State Fair

20975851R00087

Made in the USA
Lexington, KY
08 December 2018